BABY TURNS ONE

A MONTH-TO-MONTH GUIDE FOR RAISING YOUR NEWBORN BABY FROM 6 MONTHS TO A YEAR

ELIZABETH NEWBOURNE

CONTENTS

MOMMY CHECKLIST

14 Baby Essentials Every Mom Must Have...

This checklist includes:

- 14 ESSENTIALS THAT YOU DIDN'T KNOW YOU NEEDED FOR YOUR LITTLE ONE AND YOURSELF
- ITEMS WHICH WILL MAKE BEING A MAMA BEAR EASIER
- WHERE YOU CAN PURCHASE THESE ITEMS AT THE LOWEST PRICE

The last thing you want to do is be unprepared and unequipped to give your little one an enjoyable and secure environment to grow up in. It is never too late to prepare for this!

To receive your free Mommy Checklist, visit the link or scan the QR code below:

https://purelypublishing.activehosted.com/f/1

INTRODUCTION

Welcome back, mommies! Your baby is healthy and happy, and hopefully you feel less stressed about raising your little one. Wait, who am I kidding, right? I know you're still anxious that you'll do something wrong or that your tiny tot may be falling behind in reaching age-appropriate milestones. Don't worry, in *Baby Turns One*, I'll take your hand once again and guide you through the ups and downs, but this time from six-months-old to your baby's very first birthday. Big things are coming!

To all the new mommies who didn't read *Our Plus One*, I'm so glad you're joining us in the next chapter of your baby's life. Your baby is now six months old, and their personality is starting to surface, and the best news of all, it's only going to get better from here! I am honored that you chose me to walk with you through this exciting time.

Let's face it, raising a child is confusing, especially if you consider the mountains of information available out there. It's a tiresome task to wade through everything and find the most informative and professionally approved approach. For this specific reason, I decided I wanted to write pregnancy and child-rearing books—not to add to the chaos but instead, to give parents a concise yet complete guide to growing a life and nurturing their little ones after birth.

I've been where you are—three times. I spent every quiet moment I had researching everything I could about raising my child in the best possible way. Of course, I was a little more fanatical about filling my head with all the knowledge out there—child two was even more manageable, and child three was a breeze. So, that is my long way of saying I want to save you time—time you could spend catching a quick nap to recoup some energy or watch an episode of your favorite series while the baby is sleeping.

It has been my life's mission to help mothers not only take care of their children, but themselves and their relationships. Everything I share with you is based on personal experience, but most importantly, science. I have coached and guided numerous women to become supermoms, and after reading *Baby Turns One*, you'll be ready to take on the next six months with a confident smile on your face!

But before we move on to what you can expect in the next six months, I think it's a good idea to show you what you and your little one achieved in the previous six months.

Month one was a pretty stressful one—all of a sudden, you had a tiny little life in your hands. It was filled with a lot of worries, I know. You had to get used to your baby's whimpers, cries, groans, and moans and somehow decipher what they needed (at times, screaming) for. I'm sure the first month flew past so quickly, and before you knew it, your baby started to look and act more like a...well, baby.

You would've noticed an increase in strength in month two, with your baby finding it easier to lift their head somewhat. They also began to move with more control at this time as their muscles started to grow. What I remember most about month two is the constant suckling. All three of my little ones had a finger in their mouth most of the day. Remember, this is nothing to worry about—the suckling motion is very comforting for babies.

You may also have been lucky enough to receive a real smile from your little angel in month two. I know a lot of people contribute these early smiles to reflexes, gas, or cramps, but a smile in your baby's second month may be a genuine one! It's all about the timing and length—a goofy grin right after nursing will most likely be due to gas. But I am sure you could distinguish between real and forced smiles, and if you couldn't, does it even matter? Any smiling baby is beyond adorable—more so if they're your own, I know.

With the approach of month three, you would've noticed your little one is very interested in objects—their perception of colors started to improve, and it's during this time that I'm sure you pulled out the fun illustrated play mat. Talking about play, three-month-old babies just love to mimic a person's movements and expressions. Looking back, this behavior caused endless hours of entertainment in our house.

Things get even more joyful in month four when your little one turns into a real social butterfly living for attention. It's during this time when your baby starts to express their emotions more easily. On the physical front, their legs are now much stronger and will be able to take on their own body weight—with you holding them upright of course.

Their little bodies aren't so little anymore, as you may have noticed at the five-month mark. By this time they have easily doubled in size. You probably realized your baby is much more active than before, especially when they're lying on their back waiting for you to change their diaper! This is because they figured out how to roll over onto their tummies—legs and arms flying all over. You'll have to work quickly or you might get a surprise, specifically if you have a little boy.

Did you decide to switch your baby over to solids at month four or five? Or are you waiting a little longer? I hope you didn't rush! A few years ago doctors believed that month four was the perfect time to introduce solids, but they now feel it isn't set in stone. Maybe your baby enjoys milk so much, they're not ready yet? And that is okay, some babies only start eating solids at the seven or eight month mark.

Here are ways to tell your little one is ready for some delicious mashed up banana or maybe some sweet potato (American Academy of Pediatrics, n.d.)!

- There's no need for you to hold up your baby's head anymore. They're more than capable of doing it themselves while sitting in a feeding chair.
- Your little one opens their mouth when food approaches. They'll look like a cute baby bird waiting for food from mommy bird.
- It will be a game of monkey see, monkey do when it comes to dinner time as your baby mimics you when you eat. They'll even try to steal your spoon if you're close enough!
- When given a spoon, your baby will attempt to move the food into their mouth.
- Your baby weighs at least 13 pounds or double their birth weight.

You might have realized that your baby doesn't stay put anymore when you place them on the ground surrounded by some toys in month six. Babies really start to explore their environment at this time. If your baby is a little acrobat, they may be able to pull themselves into a standing position or wiggle up to sit when placed on their tummy. Again, if your baby is older than six months and still not sitting, please don't worry too much. Babies do things at their own pace, and some of them only sit unsupported at nine months.

Month six is also the time when you began brushing your baby's pearly whites. Good mouth hygiene is essential throughout your child's life, and starting early will help them keep it up as they grow. Also make sure your tiny tot has a lot of toys to chew on. Not only will this help with the teething, it's a wonderful way for them to discover the world around them—as you probably gathered since they put everything in their mouth at this age!

One thing I love about the sixth month is they really put the 'bounce' in "bouncing bundle of joy." There's no sitting on your lap anymore—your baby wants to be held in a standing position. They want to use you as their own jumping castle! This is a great exercise to strengthen your baby's legs to start walking. And it is super fun!

Mommies, as you can see, you and your baby accomplished so much over the last six months—you should feel super proud. Now it is time to prepare you for the next six months. Don't worry, in a lot of ways it is easier than the previous six months. For one, you're not as nervous anymore and have the basics under control. This means you can enjoy time with your baby stress-free!

I'm sure your baby must be fast asleep if you're reading at the moment, so get comfy and let's get started.

MONTH SIX

*a*t this point, you're a veteran of changing diapers, cleaning your baby's bottom, and moving them around (hopefully without strain). But I know there are still some questions floating around in your head, especially when it comes to switching over to solid foods—if you haven't done so earlier, or your baby's ever-changing sleeping schedule.

Not long ago, your baby was asleep more than they were awake, but from now on, they're going to require much more of your time and patience as they learn to crawl and start to explore their environment. Time flies, right? It seems like only yesterday when you held them in your arms for the first time.

Before we get started with the milestones you can

expect in month six, I just want to remind you—and this is something you should keep in mind throughout the following chapters—babies grow at different rates. *Baby Turns One* is meant as a basic guide, and you should not worry if your baby doesn't stick to what is written. Maybe they're a late bloomer —whatever the case, they usually catch up in time. However, if you are anxious that your child is taking too long or has missed out on an important milestone, speak to your doctor.

So, you've reached the halfway mark—soon, you'll be baking your little one's first birthday cake. But before then, your baby must go through some more changes.

You'll also add another aspect to your morning and evening routine: brushing teeth or maybe a tooth? Most babies will sprout their first tooth at this time, so keep a toothbrush handy!

At first, there's no need for toothpaste—a soft tooth-brush or cloth and water will work perfectly fine to remove any build-up on their teeth.

This is also the time to invest in some toys that will boost your baby's large and small motor skills, as well as intellectual, social, and language skills. Stacking toys with unique shapes and sizes or cubes of different colors work well. I found toys like cars, balls, or those that make noise work well to encourage crawling.

Your baby will also use anything and everything around them to pull themselves up. If it can get them from point A to B, they'll be even more delighted. But you don't want to limit your little one's pre-walking to using only furniture, do you? Walking toys are perfect if you want to broaden their horizons and get them mobile. These toys encourage your baby's sense of independence and promote muscle, bone, and sensory development, as well as visual-motor skills.

Pre-Walker Shoes

As your baby starts cruising around, you may want to start dressing their feet in some designer kicks, but I recommend you get them a pair of pre-walking shoes first. These shoes have soft soles and are flexible and lightweight. A 2008 study found that flexible shoes do not impair foot motion as much as regular shoes do (Wolf, et al., 2008). They come highly recommended by podiatrists because they're entirely flat, which helps your baby take their first steps.

You want to get your little one a pair of pre-walker shoes as soon as you see them standing up and trying to walk with the aid of ottomans, chairs, tables, etc. Not only do these shoes help your baby walk, but they also keep your tot's feet arm and protected. They also come with a slip-resistant bottom, which will prevent any unnecessary falls (you don't want to add to the many ones that will happen inevitably.)

That covers some of the more general changes you'll notice in your baby. Let's look at their feeding and sleep schedules and some other important transformations.

STARTING SOLIDS

I touched on this subject briefly in the introduction, but let's delve a little deeper to make sure you feel confident enough that you're making the right decision at the right time and that you're doing weaning your baby correctly. The phasing in of solid food into your baby's diet is also called complementary feeding. This is because you're entering a transitional period where your baby will still primarily rely on breast milk or formula but start learning how to eat and receive new flavors and textures.

If you understand that solid foods aren't replacing your baby's main food source at this time, then you won't be left frustrated when your baby doesn't empty a whole jar of baby food. Look at it this way: it's more about practicing to eat and exploring their sense of taste than getting much nutrition from the solid food.

Why Wait?

I mentioned that some babies would be ready for solid foods anytime from month four. Although this is the case, research shows that the ideal time is around the six-month mark (Yu, Binns & Lee, 2019). This is chiefly because your baby's digestive system is ready to deal with solid food at this time, but here are some other reasons why waiting until this time is best.

- Breast milk or formula is more than adequate in providing your little one with the energy and nutrients they need while their brain and body develops to cope with solid food. That being said, breast milk does lack iron—a vital component to your baby's growth. To combat the shortage of iron, your baby will now be ready to eat fortified cereal.

- Feeding only breast milk up until six months will protect your baby against infections and illnesses.
- Your baby will be more capable of hand-feeding themselves when they're six months old.
- They'll be more able to move food around in their mouth, chew, and swallow than earlier in their life. This means you won't always have to feed them pureed food all the time but can add roughly mashed and finger foods.

If your baby is a preemie, ask your doctor to recommend when your baby should start eating solid foods.

How to Start

When you start weaning your baby, you can give them some solid food once a day. Foods they can hold themselves are a good start, but mashed and pureed fruits or veggies fed with a spoon are also suitable. Your baby won't actually do much eating, as mentioned—it's going to be a messy job, but a fun one!

Here are nine tips to get your baby's start with solid foods off to a good start:

1. Don't give up! Remember, your little one is learning a new skill, and while some may accept solid foods quickly, others may take longer.
2. Don't rush. Give your baby enough time to explore and enjoy this new phenomenon. Pick a time that suits both of you; when you don't have to be somewhere and your tiny tot isn't too tired.
3. Encourage your little one to eat, and when they do put food in their mouth, show your excitement. Praise them when they do things right, and you'll motivate them to do it more often.
4. Go at their pace. Follow your baby's cues; they will let you know when they're hungry or have had enough. My girl used to close her mouth firmly when she had her fill and no "here comes the choo choo train" could make her budge. Babies will also turn their

heads away slightly or with force when they've had enough. If you see these signs, stop. Never force your little one to eat. Instead, wait until the next feeding.

5. Patience is key. At first, it may seem as if your baby doesn't like the food on offer, but don't give up. It may take quite a few times for them to get used to the new tastes and textures. Each of my children didn't like broccoli at first (predictable, I know), but after ten or more tries, we had success, and they still eat it to this day. On some days, your little one will eat more; on others, they'll eat less. Then there will be the days where you can stand on your head, and they still won't eat anything at all. This behavior is nothing to worry about; it's perfectly normal.

6. Be okay with your baby making a mess. I know we've been taught not to play with our food, but when your baby is just starting to eat, throw that rule out the window. You want them to touch and hold their food and feed themselves—even if that means cleaning mashed pumpkin off of most surfaces when they're done. You will

see that your little one will try to take the spoon from you, give it to them, and allow them to feed themselves.

7. Switch off the television and keep any other distractions to a minimum when your baby is eating.

8. Show them how to eat. As you read earlier, babies this age like to mimic other people. It is a good idea to eat meals together, so they have the opportunity to see how you eat.

9. Offer your baby food before milk. Your little one won't be too interested in the food if they just had their milk meal.

Continue to give your six-month-old about 24 to 40 oz (five cups) of breastmilk divided over four to seven feedings. If you give your little one formula, they will most likely drink at the lower end of the breast milk quantity. You can also boil and cool some water to quench their thirst, but only give it to them after they finish their milk. You don't want to fill their bellies up with something that will take the space of something nutritious.

Also, your baby won't need three square meals a day. They have tiny tummies and offering them a teaspoon of food or a few small pieces once a day will be more than enough.

Before we have a look at the perfect first foods, here's an equipment checklist with everything you'll need to make feeding time as stress-free as possible.

- High chair. Secure your baby in a straight-up position and never leave them unattended.
- Plastic bibs. It's going to be messy chaos at first, so to make sure you don't have to change your baby into clean clothes after each meal, use a plastic or pelican bib.
- Soft spoon. Your baby's coordination isn't fully developed yet, and there will be a lot of trial and error when they first learn to use a spoon. Weaning spoons will lessen the blow and be much gentler on their gums.
- Plastic bowl. I recommend you get a weaning-specific bowl that has a suction base; otherwise, you'll spend most of the meal time wiping food off the floor.
- Messy mat. It's easier to clean the mess your baby will make when eating if you use

a messy mat or some newspaper under the high chair. All the flying food bits will land on it, and it is easy to pick up—removing the need to mop the floor after each feeding.

First Foods

When it comes to your baby's first food, it is recommended that you start with a single vegetable or fruit. Personally, I believe starting with finger food is the best approach. This will give them the chance to touch, hold, and explore their food. Furthermore, they can go at their own pace as they learn to feed themselves. Self-feeding is also an excellent way for baby to develop their fine motor skills and hand-eye coordination. Cut up food in large enough sizes for your baby to hold in a fist with a little bit sticking out.

You can use your finger as a size guide. Don't give your baby anything that is a choking hazard; raw carrots, apples, and nuts are some examples of food to avoid. Instead, give them soft cooked vegetables or fruit.

Here is a list of finger foods:

- Cooked carrot, broccoli, butternut, parsnip, and cauliflower.
- Steamed or soft fruits like apple, peach, melon, and banana.
- Avocado cut into pieces they can hold.
- Cooked starches such as potato, sweet potato, pasta, noodles, etc.
- Fish without bones.
- Deboned chicken or lamb, cooked until soft.
- Hard-boiled eggs.
- Sticks of pasteurized cheese.

You can either stick to finger foods or you can combine it with spoon-feeding pureed or mashed foods. A lot of parents prefer only to feed finger foods. This method is known as baby-led weaning. There really is no right or wrong way. As long as your baby is eating a variety of food, they'll get all the nutrients they need no matter the method you use.

For both methods, you want to keep the following in mind:

- Start with a single vegetable or fruit and add something new every few days.
- Include veggies that aren't sweet. Feeding them a variety of vegetables (and not just sweeter ones like carrots or pumpkin) may help prevent them from being fussy eaters later on in life.
- Don't add any sugar.
- Cool food down entirely before you give it to your baby.
- Introduce food containing allergens one at a time and in small amounts. It will make it easier to pinpoint the culprit should your little one have a reaction.

Food Allergies

In the past, it was common practice to delay giving babies foods that contain allergens in the hopes of preventing allergies. This, however, is not the case any longer. The Dietary Guidelines Advisory Committee (2020) now recommends introducing allergenic foods as early as four months after studies found that early consumption of these foods may reduce a baby's chances of developing a food allergy. Just be sure to introduce these foods one at a time and when you're close-by to observe your little one.

Only around 8% of children in America are affected by food allergies, and it shouldn't be taken lightly (Gupta, et al., 2018). Bad reactions to food include gassiness, diarrhea, vomiting, runny nose, watery eyes, rashes, wheezing, and overall crankiness.

If your baby displays any of these symptoms after trying a known allergen for the first time, make a note to speak to your doctor before offering it to them again. The same applies if there is a history of allergies in your family. In addition, should your baby react negatively to most of the new food you add to their diet, seek medical attention immediately.

Safety and Hygiene

You don't want to put your baby at risk of getting food-borne diseases when you introduce solid foods.

Here are some food safety and hygiene tips to help you safeguard your little one against germs.

- Wash your hands before working with food.
- Wipe and disinfect the work surface.
- Rinse all raw fruits and veggies.
- Don't give your baby any foods that are hard or contain pips, stones, or bones, i.e., avoid anything that is a choking hazard.
- Cut grapes, cherry tomatoes, and other small and round food into smaller pieces.
- Don't leave your baby unsupervised when they're eating.

Stop Your Baby From Choking

It may be difficult to distinguish between gagging and choking when you first introduce solid foods. Most babies will gag while learning to eat—it's a way to regulate the amount of food they can put in their mouth at one time.

Signs that your baby is gagging include:

- Watering eyes
- Tongue pushing forward

- Retching to bring food forward in their mouth
- Vomiting

If your baby suddenly starts coughing after eating something, there's a chance that they're choking. It doesn't matter how careful you are, choking is always a possibility.

To help a choking child, do the following:

1. Remove the object if you can see it, but be sure not to make things worse by pushing the food further down their airway.
2. Put your baby face down along your thighs while you're in a sitting position while supporting their head with your one hand.
3. Use the heel of your hand to give five sharp back blows between your little one's shoulder blades.
4. If this is ineffective, but your child is still conscious, try giving chest thrusts to increase pressure in their chest, which will help displace the object.

To do a chest thrust:

1. Turn your baby face-up along the length of your thighs.
2. Locate your little one's breastbone and put two fingers in the middle.
3. Push down five times and compress the chest by about a third each time.

If this doesn't work, but your baby is still conscious, continue with the back blows and chest thrusts. In the event that you're alone with your baby but there is someone else in the house, call out for help. This person can proceed to call emergency response. If you're completely on your own, get to a phone and call for help, but do not leave your baby alone. Continue with the back blow and chest thrust cycle until help arrives.

Should your child lose consciousness from choking, place them on a flat and firm surface and call for help. Use your speakerphone since you'll want both hands free to administer CPR.

Your Solid Food Questions Answered

I've helped a lot of mommies transition their little ones to solid foods. They had a lot of anxiety at first, but they were more at ease after we covered some of their burning questions. In this section, I will answer some of the most-asked questions new moms ask when it is time to introduce their baby to solid food.

Why is my baby making unpleasant faces while eating?

Babies are well-known for strange faces in reaction to tasting new food. A study was done to see if there was a relationship between babies' facial expressions and their food. Researchers offered babies pureed green beans for the first time, and their disgust was visible (Forestell & Mennella, 2017).

The most common facial expressions noted include:

- 95% squinted
- 82% wiggled their brows
- 76% raised their upper lips
- 42% wrinkled their noses

As you can imagine, the more repulsed they were, the more slowly they ate. But this doesn't mean you should stop giving your baby foods they don't like at first. The same study found that babies get over their initial dislike of foods—it just takes time. After offering the tiny participants in the study pureed green beans for eight days in a row, they were eating almost three times as much as the first time.

If you find your baby doesn't like a specific food, keep trying. I recommend waiting a few minutes after your baby first pushes away a particular food before you bring the spoon up to their mouth again. Try this three times, and if they're still not interested in eating what's on the menu, best to try another day.

My baby keeps pushing the food out with their tongue. Why do they do that?

That's not unusual behavior at all. Your baby is still experiencing the tongue-thrust reflex (Healthline, n.d.). This reflex— the tongue pushes forward as soon as the mouth is stimulated—works great when your baby is still suckling but isn't helpful when they start to eat solid foods. So, instead of the food being moved to the back of the throat, it will end up everywhere but inside their mouth.

Also, keep in mind that your baby is still learning to eat and don't have the necessary skills yet. Just keep going—your baby needs the practice!

What should I do when my baby keeps grabbing the spoon?

Mealtime will, most of the time, turn into a messy affair. You don't only have their tongue-thrust reflex to deal with, but their curiosity too. Your little one wants to examine everything at this age, and that includes the spoon you're trying to feed them with!

You have two options when this happens. First, you can keep adding spoons to the mix. If your baby shows interest in one spoon, give it to them and continue to feed them with another one. They may switch their focus from the spoon in their hand to the one you're using. When that happens, you can give it to them and take yet another one to feed them with. Both your baby's hands will be occupied, and they may be less distracted by what you're holding in yours.

That being said, some babies are so curious, they'll keep taking spoons out of your hand until you have none left. If that is the case, you have the option of loading a spoon with food and giving them free rein. You can leave them to attempt guiding the spoon to their mouth, or you can help them out. The bottom line is: don't get frustrated. Your baby won't starve when they don't ingest a lot of the food during these feedings. As mentioned earlier, at this time, it's all about learning, so let them explore and play as much as they want.

There will be a lot of cleaning to do afterward for mommy, but the more they practice, the sooner the day will arrive where they can eat independently without making (much of) a mess.

When can I start feeding my baby lumpy foods?

Your baby will be learning about food textures as well as they discover the wonderful flavors of solid foods. You can start to introduce more lumpy types of food at the six-month mark. I know they don't have teeth at this time, but don't worry; your baby will be able to mash soft and lumpy foods with their gums. They'll also give their chewing muscles a good workout as they chew lumpy foods.

Your baby should be familiar with clumpy foods before nine months—research found that they're less likely to be fussy eaters if they're exposed to textured food before this time (Coulthard, Harris & Emmet, 2009).

One word of caution: taste the food before you give it to your little one to make sure the lumps aren't too hard, and you can easily squash it between your tongue and the roof of your mouth. If the food is too hard, it can be a choking hazard.

Is there anything I can do to avoid raising a picky eater?

Well, the previous point is a good start, but you have to keep in mind that while you can make a difference, you can't control your baby's taste buds completely (Beauchamp & Mennella, 2009).

One of the best ways to influence what your little one likes is through breast milk. What you eat changes the taste of your milk, and your baby will prefer these flavors. This is the best way to 'program' your baby to enjoy a wider range of foods.

Another tip I can give you is to resist giving your baby only their favorite foods. Make an effort to introduce them to new food on a regular basis, especially vegetables that they may take a while to accept.

Homemade Baby Food

As a qualified nutritionist, I'm a big advocate for making baby food at home. There are so many hidden preservatives, hidden sugars, additives, and other unsafe ingredients in store-bought baby food that aren't beneficial to your little one's health. If you cook your baby's food, you will know exactly what you put in and can make sure you only give them the best. That's not the only reason why homemade baby food should be your number one choice, it's also:

- Freezer-friendly
- Easy and quick to make
- Packed with nutritional value
- Cheaper than store-bought baby food

What's more, you only need three ingredients or less!

Also, when it comes to making baby food at home, don't think you have to give your baby bland, flavorless food—babies actually enjoy flavors like garlic! Remember, your little one was exposed to all the flavors you as a mother ate while they were still in your tummy (Dewar, n.d.)! And as you already read, the food you eat flavors your breast milk. Of course, that doesn't mean you should use spice with reckless abandon—babies don't tolerate bitter flavors and spicy irritants.

YOUR BABY'S SENSES

Your little one's senses are much sharper than they were a short while ago. You may have noticed that their eyes have changed color! If your baby had lighter-colored eyes, they may have changed over time and will now settle on their final shade. If your baby still has the same blue eyes they came into the world with, chances are they'll stay just that way! Let's have a closer look at all the senses.

Sound. Your little one will be able to identify yours and other familiar voices and sounds. It's during this time you should read to your baby as often as possible—it will help their language development tremendously. They will also respond to you in their own voice from now on, and although their words aren't complete, their baby talk is a lot more sophisticated. Where the vowel sounds started around three months, they'll start throwing in consonants at this time.

Vision. Your baby is now able to see things from farther away—and in more detail. Their vision is becoming sharper and clearer, and you should give them a variety of colorful toys to stimulate their senses. They can also now recognize your face and will most probably greet you with a smile when they see you walking into a room. You will even notice them staring at you as they inspect your features. Since they have an understanding of "object permanence"— they realize a dropped object hasn't disappeared but is just out of sight—now is the time to play peek-a-boo. They will giggle with excitement as your face reappears from behind your hands.

Touch. Your little one's general curiosity extends to touch. Where they loved to touch your skin, they now want to explore different textures. They want to experience new sensations, so give them various objects and surfaces to inspect with their hands.

Taste. We covered this sense quite in-depth in the previous section.

Smell. For a while now, your baby has been able to recognize your scent, as well as other familiar smells. Now at six-months, they'll begin to distinguish between other smells too.

SLEEP TIME

Your baby is cute as a button at six months with their gummy smiles, babbling, and continued giggling. But as adorable as your little one is, their sleeping pattern is changing, and no amount of cute can fix the sleepless nights you may soon experience. Your little one's sleep pattern at this time can be described in one word: baffling. Where they slept soundly the last month or two, their sleep pattern will get a little unpredictable around this time.

Your baby should be getting 15 hours of sleep a day —two or three naps plus nine to 11 hours of sleep at night. If your tiny tot sleeps like a dream and sticks to a schedule, then you're one of the lucky ones. Some parents will have to deal with cranky, sleep-deprived babies who seemingly forgot how to sleep.

Sleep Regression

All of a sudden, it may seem as if your little one doesn't know what sleep is—they don't sleep through the night anymore and puts up a fuss when it's time for a nap. They may be going through what is known as sleep regression.

Many babies will experience this around four months, but they're also expected at the six-month mark. This temporary interruption of their sleeping routine often goes hand-in-hand with developmental milestones. They're more physically active during the day as they roll around, attempt to crawl, stand up against the furniture, etc. This will leave them feeling exhausted and excited at the same time— they'll be so revved up to practice their new skills that they'll struggle to fall asleep.

Then, of course, there's teething, which will no doubt disrupt your baby's sleep.

Possible Problems

Let's look at all the possible sleep problems your baby may experience at this time.

Teething: It's a painful process to get teeth, and although you may not be able to spot a new pearly white doesn't mean one isn't trying to break through. If your baby is cranky, drooling, and pulling their ears, you may want to give them a teething ring to alleviate the itch that goes with teething and to help things along.

Night waking: You heaved a sigh of relief when your baby finally started to sleep through the night. Now, it's back! You may have to try sleep training to teach them to fall asleep with little or no help from mommy or daddy. Something else that may be waking your little one up during the night is hunger. So, if you want them to sleep through, make sure they get enough to eat throughout the day. I used to wake all three of my babies before bed for an extra feeding, and when they did wake up hungry at night, I kept the nursing sessions short and made it extra boring. Keep the lights off, don't talk to them too much, and don't sing except for soft lullabies—you don't want them to think nighttime is playtime.

Early rising: When your baby wakes up with the birds, you may want to check that no light is peeking through the curtains. Your little one's biological clock is starting to fall in with nature, so you have to trick it a little. Hang some blackout curtains and make sure there aren't any early morning distractions that will wake them—of course, if your neighbor decides to mow the lawn at 7 am, there's not much you or your baby can do!

General fussiness: It's fun to be six months old! Your baby is discovering new things about themselves and the world daily—no wonder they don't want to go to sleep; they don't want to miss out. To help calm them down, I suggest you set up a routine and stick to it consistently. It may take awhile for your little one to get used to the routine, but if you push through, you'll be rewarded with a drowsy baby who is ready for a good night's sleep.

Although there's no one-size-fits all routine for six-month-old babies, here's a sample sleep schedule you can adapt to suit your family.

- 7:00 am: Wake up
- 8:45 am: Take a morning nap
- 10:45 am: Wake up
- 12:30 pm: Time for another nap
- 2:00 pm: Wake up

- 4:00 pm: Take an afternoon nap
- 4:30 pm: Wake up
- 6:30 pm: Bedtime routine, for example, take a bath, brush teeth, read a book
- 7:00 pm: Time for bed

Sleep Tips

Routine and consistency: I know you're so tired you're just about ready to fall over spontaneously for some shut-eye. Unfortunately, your baby is not on the same page—they'd much rather stay up and discover the world. To help your baby calm down, stick to a bedtime routine so your little one's brain will get the message that it's time to wind down.

Keep it cozy: A few weeks ago, your baby would fall asleep anywhere. Those days are over. They are much more aware of their environment at this age, so you have to create one that is conducive to sleep. Keep their bedroom dark and quiet, and at a temperature that isn't too hot or cold—the sweet spot lies between 68 and 72 degrees. If you want, you can use a white noise machine in your little one's room to cancel out noises that may disturb their peace.

Naps are important: You may have to adjust your schedule around your baby's naps to make sure they don't miss out on this much-needed rest. You don't want your little one to be over-tired when it's bedtime—they'll be cranky, and it won't be easy to get them to sleep. Also, when they sleep during the day, encourage them to sleep in their crib.

Get active: A busy baby will be a tired baby when it's time for bed. The more active your little one is throughout the day, the better the chances they'll fall asleep without protest. Play peek-a-boo, let them crawl all over, bop them up and down on your lap while in a standing position, or think of other activities that will tire them out.

As you can imagine, sleep is vital for the healthy growth of your baby. So, to recap:

- Make sure your baby takes two or three naps a day and sleeps up to 11 hours at night.
- Follow a sleep-schedule.
- Consistently stick to a bedtime routine.
- Limit any distractions in your little one's room.

- Create a calm and peaceful environment.

TIME FOR A BATH

I hope you're excited—mommy and baby can finally take a bath together! Your little one is ready at six months to brave deeper waters—that is, if they can sit well on their own. Although you don't have to be with them in the tub, it's so much fun, I won't be surprised if you're more excited about bath time than they are! With these tips in mind, the transition will be smooth sailing:

Safety First

Never leave your baby alone—not even for a split second. It doesn't matter if you're using a tub seat or a ring; your baby can still slip under water. The first thing you need to do is prevent your baby's bum from slipping and sliding all over the tub. A skid-free bath mat or towel will keep their bottom where it should be. Secondly, make sure you have all the supplies you'll need within arm's reach. If you have to get something from another room, do not leave your baby alone. Instead, wrap them in a towel and take them with you—the bath isn't going anywhere. I recommend you buy a faucet cover to protect your baby's head if they bump into it by accident.

Test the Waters

Always test the water temperature with your elbow or wrist before you put your baby in the tub. The water should never be hotter than 120 degrees F. You also don't want to overfill the tub. Start with an inch or two of water at first—you can add more as your baby gets better control over their body.

Take Things Slow

Wade in—not just for your baby's sake, but yours. I suggest you place the little tub inside the big empty tub a few times during bath time. Not only will you get used to washing your baby in a tub that is intimidating you—your tiny tot will get used to being inside this new space.

It's a big jump from a small, constricting baby bath to a huge bathtub; this won't go unnoticed by your baby. It may be particularly scary if your little one isn't fond of taking baths in the first place. If you're been using a European-style tub that has a tight, comfortable fit with a lot of back support, your little one will feel even more out of place in a wide-open tub. Do your best to familiarize your baby with the new environment. You can use a bath seat to make the transition more comfortable, which will also prevent baby from lying down in the water and make them feel more secure in general.

Don't Forget the Toys

Make it fun! There's no need for you to buy a fleet of expensive water toys—plastic cups and containers that can float and be filled with water will provide your little dipper with boat-loads of fun. Of course, don't forget a rubber ducky to keep your tiny tot company in the tub.

Choose Tear-Free Products

Nothing will put your baby off of getting their hair rinsed as quickly as burning eyes. I recommend you use tear-free products for as long as you can to prevent soap suds from getting into your splash-happy baby's eyes.

Your little one won't only scream and cry should they experience the burning and stinging from soap in the eyes, but they will also lose trust in mommy, and sometimes hard to regain in this arena.

Take Care of Your Back

You will most likely experience back strain every time you bath your tiny tot in the big tub. If you have a sensitive back, you can consider investing in a special sling for bath time, which will make it possible for you and your little one to shower together while reducing the stress on your back. If you're not a fan of that idea, the bathroom or kitchen sink is an option if your baby still fits. You'll be able to stand, saving wear and tear on your back. Alternatively, keep bath time as short as possible—just long enough to get the job done.

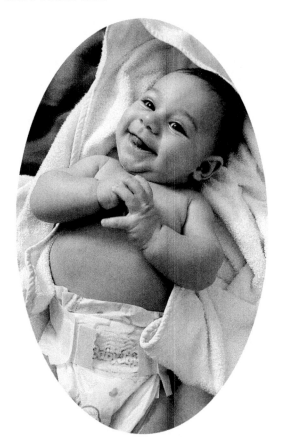

DIAPER DYNAMICS

As your baby transitions to solid foods, you may notice a few surprises when it comes to Number 2. Your little one will poop less, stools will be thicker, and you may see certain foods passed through undigested—which is expected since babies don't always chew their food well. You may also have to deal with a constipated baby if they've been eating rice cereal fortified with iron. Other foods may also cause your baby to get backed up.

A baby's diaper is filled with a lot of mystery, especially in the early months. But you've spent enough time looking at it and cleaning it up to have a general idea of what is normal and what isn't.

At this age, it's not so much about how many times your baby goes potty and more about the poop's consistency. If it's hard when it comes out, it may point to constipation, and that is something you don't want your baby to be.

How to Tell Your Baby Is Constipated

If you inspect your baby's diaper and their poop is thicker than toothpaste or looks like marbles, then your little one is probably constipated. Your baby will also seem uncomfortable and may strain when then go number two.

This happens for various reasons: it can be due to not drinking enough fluids, the transition to solid foods, and the type of food they're eating. Luckily there aren't only foods that cause constipation but alleviate it too.

You can give your little one two to four ounces of prune, pear, or apple juice to soften their stools. The sugar in the juice draws water into the bowel, and this helps to soften the stool. If your baby doesn't respond to just the juice, you can add barley or oatmeal cereal, plums, prunes, peaches, and apricots to their diet until they poop normally again. Don't eliminate bananas, rice, and other foods high in soluble fibers (binding foods); just cut back on them.

I recommend you check with your pediatrician before you give your little one any home remedies for constipation, especially when you're considering the use of laxatives, mineral oil, or enemas. I know it's not nice to see your baby strain or grunt as they poop, but don't be fooled—it takes more than a groan and some extra effort to signal constipation. Remember, your little one has to poop lying down, so their bodies will have to work a little harder to get things done. You can pick your baby up and hold their knees against their chest to get gravity to help them out a little.

There isn't much you can do to prevent constipation, so best prepare yourself to recognize the warning signs and deal with them accordingly. Most babies will experience bouts of constipation as they grow, but it usually passes without any medical intervention. However, if you are concerned, talk to your doctor.

What About Diarrhea?

Thin, watery stool streaked with mucus usually indicates your baby has diarrhea. That combined with you having to change their diaper more often than usual. Antibiotics, milk allergies, too much fruit juice, or gastroenteritis can all cause runny poop.

When your baby has loose stools, your only focus should be to keep them hydrated with breast milk or formula and even some pediatric electrolyte solutions when you can't keep up with all the diaper changes.

Only when you notice signs of dehydration—dry lips, sunken eyes or fontanels (soft spots)—should you worry and get medical advice.

When to Call the Doctor

I know you may be tempted to call your baby's doctor every time you spot any changes in their diaper, but you can relax. Your baby's poop is going to change in shape, color, and smell as your little one grows. The only times when you should get immediate medical advice is when:

- Your baby's poop is white (not enough bile), black (blood in the stomach or small intestine), or streaked with red (blood from colon or rectum).
- Your little one screams in pain while pooping, or you can see blood.
- There's mucus in your baby's poop, which may signal an infection or food intolerance.
- Their poop changes dramatically after they eat something new. This may be a sign of a food allergy.

There you have it mommies—we made it to the end of month six, and now it's time to discover what exciting things await you and your little one in month seven!

MONTH SEVEN

*H*ave you noticed you, all of the sudden, have a comedian in the house? At month seven, your little one's sense of humor is starting to emerge, which will make for many laughs. Your baby may also be crawling all over the place if they're the ambitious type! But don't stress if they're still only creeping around, crawling is not on this month's list of must-dos. Usually, babies who had plenty of tummy time will start crawling earlier, while those who spent less time on their tummies will crawl at around month nine or so.

If your baby is part of the early bloomers, keep in mind that there's no one correct way to crawl. Your baby will have their own crawling style—some may even crawl backward or sideways! It's not how they get from point A to B that is important.

The seven-month mark for most babies is a transitional age: they'll have some mobility but not enough to get into any real trouble. The ability to see a toy and not being able to get it themselves may lead to frustration, so get ready to deal with some protest and tantrums. Don't be too quick to help them, no matter how tempting it may be. It's from challenges like these that your baby will develop skills that will benefit them.

All in all, your little one is learning to be much more independent—they can sit unassisted, reach for and pick up toys they want; they can hold and drink from a sippy cup, and may even be able to use a spoon.

Your baby is also steadily moving up the growth charts, gaining up to 1 ¼ pounds and growing between ½ and ¾ inch in length in one month! Your little one will keep up this incredible growth with a steady diet of breast milk or formula and solids. Baby is becoming a more experienced eater, and where they once only ate one to two teaspoons of solid food, your little muncher will now easily be able to eat anywhere from four to nine tablespoons per day. This helps a lot when it comes to the weight gain department.

Let's look at some other interesting facts about your baby at this time in their life.

They love repetition. I know this is not something you want to read. Who wants to hear the same song over and over, right? Well, your little one is going to ask you to sing or play a song a thousand times, and when you're done, they'll ask for it a thousand times more. Unfortunately (for your ears), their love of repetition will continue up to preschool age. The reason why they want to hear something time and time again is because of the predictability. Knowing what happens next gives them a sense of power and mastery: "Look mom, I know what is going to happen next! See how smart I am."

They will start to clap their hands. This milestone is worth celebrating with much fanfare! The fact that your baby can bring their two hands together means their hand-eye coordination and fine-motor skills are developing adequately. These are the skills your baby will later use to catch a ball and hold a pencil. One way to get your baby clapping is by doing it yourself. It's contagious! So, whenever your tiny tot does something worth cheering for, clap your hands and excitedly praise them. Soon they'll start to clap all on their own.

Your baby is turning into a master communicator. You'll be happy to read that your baby can now understand what 'no' means, but I can't guarantee that they'll actually listen when you say it! They can also recognize their name and will respond when you say it. But what is most impressive is your baby's nonverbal communication skills. Not only will they surprise you with a variety of expressions, but they will be able to tell how you're feeling by your tone of voice and facial expressions.

Before we look at the more critical aspects of month seven, here are some tips to make this time more special for mommy and baby.

- Make your little one part of mealtimes. Push their high chair up to the dinner table for some bonding time over a nice plate of food. Since they have some control over a spoon, you can enjoy your meal while they help themselves to some delicious (hopefully homemade) baby food.

- Every day should have playtime planned into it. Go down memory lane and use some staples from your own childhood. Peek-a-boo, this little piggy, and itsy-bitsy spider are wonderful ways to entertain and stimulate your baby.

- Baby proofing the house is essential at this time. Your baby will soon be mobile, and you don't want them to get hurt. Get down on their level and make sure the play areas are safe. I will discuss baby proofing in detail later on in this chapter.

Okay, let's get down to the more serious business of month seven.

FEEDING TIME

As your baby grows, they will start eating less during the day, and they'll move toward eating only three meals a day—breakfast, lunch, tea—while still enjoying their usual milk feeds. Since they're eating more solid foods, their appetite for milk will slowly decline; they may skip a milk feed altogether. So, don't worry as your baby adapts to their meals according to how much solid food they're eating.

As you gradually increase the variety of food your baby consumes, their energy and nutrient needs won't primarily be met by breastmilk or formula anymore.

To ensure your little one gets everything they need for their body to function optimally and to carry them through growth spurts, their diet should include the following:

- Meat, fish, fortified breakfast cereals, leafy green vegetables, beans and lentils, and other foods high in iron. Your baby should get 11 mg of iron a day. This mineral is vital in the production of hemoglobin, which carries oxygen through the body. It also helps brain development—something that happens non-stop as your child learns new motor skills and memory.
- A variety of colorful fruits and vegetables. Don't forget the ones with bitter flavors: broccoli, cauliflower, cabbage, and spinach.

- Starchy foods like potatoes, bread, rice, and pasta.
- Plain yogurt and low-sodium cheese. All dairy should be full-fat and pasteurized.
- Aim for 24 to 30 ounces breast milk or formula a day, four to nine tablespoons of fruit and veggies and starches, as well as one to six tablespoons of protein.

Note: Since your baby is under age one, they're not allowed to eat honey or drink cow's milk and fruit juice.

Ready-Made vs Homemade Baby Food

You already know that I am a big proponent of home-made baby food, but I want you to make up your own mind. Furthermore, I don't want you to feel judged should you decide to go with the store-bought option —both choices have pros and cons.

If you dig a little, you'll actually find some conflicting views. One group says homemade meals leads to obesity, while the other believes the hidden sugar and trans fats in ready-made foods are far worse than the extra calories DIY baby food contains.

Scientists compared 278 ready-made meals with 409 home-cooked meals gathered from cookbooks (Carstairs et al., 2016). The study found that home-made meals were cheaper but higher in dietary fat, with 50% of the recipes containing more energy than recommended. They were also higher in carbohydrates, salt, protein, fat and saturated fat.

This must mean shop-bought baby food is healthier, right?

Well, not entirely. Homemade food contains between seven and 200% more nutrients depending on which brand you buy. Yes, ready-made meals may be healthier than initially thought, but they still contain more sugar and are less nutritious in some cases. You really have to study the labels between brands to make sure you pick the best one.

In the study previously mentioned, researchers noted that relying solely on commercial baby food would mean your child would be exposed to limited food types.

As you can see, the jury is still out on whether your own concoctions are the healthiest option for your baby, but there's no harm in going the home cooked route or even combining the two. The main culprits when cooking for your little one are salt, sugar, and fat. If you add these to the dishes you make, it makes home cooked food unhealthy.

Still, it is good to know that when you are pressed for time, the baby food in stores is more nutritious than initially thought.

Let's sum up the pros and cons.

Ready-Made Baby Food

Pros

Convenience: It's quick to grab a jar of food off of a shelf—you don't have to spend time in the kitchen preparing the meal yourself.

Portability: You don't have to worry about containers with loose lids spilling in your bag—the jars are sealed tightly and can easily be transported in a diaper bag. All you need is a spoon, and dinner is served no matter where you are. Furthermore, there's no need to hunt for a fridge when you're not home; you don't have to worry about refrigerating store-bought baby food until it is opened.

Nourishing: Although some brands aren't as nutritious as others, there is store-bought baby food that offers your baby all they need. Overall, research shows ready-made foods are healthier than many believe.

Cons

Expensive: You're paying for brand names and packaging, especially if you're going for the best of the best, and in the end, this will cost you way more than homemade alternatives.

Waste: Not all packaging is environmentally friendly or recyclable.

Preservatives and additives: Ready-made baby food contains various listed or unlisted preservatives to make the food shelf-stable (more on this later). These preservatives aren't healthy for your baby. I recommend looking for organic baby foods that use Vitamin C as a preservative and have to be grown without using pesticides (if they want to stay certified organic.)

Contaminants: Some baby foods have been recalled due to contaminants. Not only can it show up in the water used to cook the food in, but the packaging itself can also contain harmful substances —like lead, for instance.

Homemade Baby Food

Pros

You know what is in the food: There's no hidden ingredients when you make your baby's food. Furthermore, you can make almost anything you eat into baby food—just skip the salt and limit the seasoning.

Cost: It's less expensive than store-bought baby food. You may have to invest in a blender or food processor initially, but that's the only real expense you'll have when you go the home cooked route.

Variety: There's no need to open multiple jars to feed your little one a variety of foods. You can combine foods and concoct your own delicious meals that will cater to all your baby's nutritional needs.

Very nutritious: As you read earlier, DIY baby food can contain up to 200% more nutrients than its store-bought counterpart.

Cons

Safety: Ready-made baby food is pasteurized, which kills off bacteria. The same doesn't apply to homemade baby food, and you will have to take extra precautions when working with the food to make sure it doesn't get contaminated.

Storage: Homemade baby food doesn't keep as well since it contains no preservatives (unless you use vitamin C). With that being said, you can freeze the dishes as long as you store them in small batches that don't have to be thawed and frozen continuously.

What Does Shelf-Stable Mean?

The fact of the matter is, it's challenging to bring fresh food to supermarkets without sacrificing something along the way. If you think about it, all store-bought baby food has the same texture and consistency, and even the colors will be close to identical between similar fruits and veggies. In nature, that's not quite how things work—there are slight variants in color and taste between one apple and the next. That means companies have to add a lot of unnatural ingredients to keep things consistent.

One of the main additives is preservatives to keep the products shelf-stable. This means baby food can sit on supermarket shelves for up to two years without refrigeration or spoilage. Unfortunately, in addition to preservatives, the food is highly processed to remove anything that may cause the food to go bad, but the same process also eliminates a lot of the good stuff.

The high levels of heat used is the main culprit for breaking down vitamins and destroying vital enzymes that help with digestion. In the end, all you're left with is a syrupy jam that contains more sugar than real nutritional value.

So, shelf-stability means you will get unspoiled baby food that tastes great for baby (sugar, sugar, sugar) but doesn't have the best nutritional value. No wonder your little one doesn't want to eat home cooked veggies after enjoying jarred baby food.

Now, I don't want to sound like a Debbie Downer, but I have a distinct gripe with baby food pouches. I know they're labelled as organic, claims to be filled with fiber, and reads "good for your baby's brain," so how can they be bad for your little one?

The Problem With Baby Pouches

I know they seem like a godsend when you're busy and your baby is screaming for something to eat. And yes, they're fine when used in moderation, but the fact that these pouches account for 25% of baby food sales in America is worrying (Nielsen's Total Food View, 2018).

They may seem like a combination of convenience and healthful nutrition at the twist of a cap, but this is where the problem lies. When these pouches make up most of a baby's daily meals, they miss out on vital developmental skills, and the pouches may contribute to bad snacking habits and overeating.

Some colleagues of mine have noted delays in motor development among children who eat predominately from pouches. These tiny tots only learned to self-feed with a spoon later in life. This may not seem like a major problem, but it does mean these children miss out on the exciting stage of food exploration.

As you read earlier, your child needs to be able to make a mess when they eat. This curiosity will lead to healthy food habits and prevent your child from becoming a picky eater. If they don't have the opportunity to smear food all over their face and then attempt to lick it off while waving a spoon around and solely rely on pouches, they will, later on, be dependent on their parents to spoon-feed them.

Babies use all their senses when they first discover solid food. Being able to see, smell, and touch food increases their acceptance of new foods (Dazeley & Houston-Price, 2014; Coulthard et al., 2017).

Another concern about pouched food is the high sugar content. Research has shown that most commercial baby food, including pouches, is blended with sweet fruits and veggies (Moding et al., 2018). You can imagine that these sweet ingredients bump up these products' sugar content by quite a lot. What's worse, pouched purees are even higher in sugar than jarred baby food (Beauregard et al., 2019). For example, pouches contain around 11 grams of sugar per serving—that's a whopping two tablespoons! That puts your little one on the road to tooth decay, and worse, obesity.

Regrettably, a lot of parents use these sugar-laden pouches to get their little ones to stop whining. This is concerning since irritable children may associate sweet snacks with calming down, leading to emotional eating later in life.

As you can see, there are several reasons why over-doing pouch feeding is a problem. There is nothing wrong with giving your baby the occasional pouch when you're caught in the middle of nowhere and don't have a spoon to opt for the healthier option: jarred baby food. However, it becomes problematic when you rely on pouch food daily. I know you don't want to choose convenience over your little one's health, so now that you're better informed, you can make the best choice for your growing baby.

BREASTFEEDING AT SEVEN MONTHS

You know milk should remain a part of your baby's diet even though they are starting to eat solids, but that doesn't mean you have to continue breastfeeding. Since your tiny tot can drink from a sippy cup, using a breast pump is an option from the seven-month mark onward.

What do those in the know say about when to stop breastfeeding? Well, according to the World Health

Organization (2020), you should breastfeed for two years and beyond. In fact, if you look at it from an anthropological perspective, the optimal duration to breastfeed your child is between two-and-a-half and seven years old. However, cultural norms have caused mommies to wean their young at a much younger age (Dettwyler, 2004).

But what benefits are there to breastfeeding for longer?

Nutritional Value

We already established that your little one still needs breast milk even as they start to transition to solid foods. Since they're only now learning how to eat, they won't get a lot of nutritional value from food. Breast milk lacks iron, zinc, and vitamins B and D, but it provides your little one with protein, vitamin C, vitamin A, folate, and vitamin B12.

Medicinal Value

Breastfeeding for longer than what is considered "culturally appropriate" lowers your baby's chances of some childhood and illnesses. It also helps them recover more quickly should they get ill. The health benefits of breastfeeding are so comprehensive that you can consider it a form of "personalized medicine" with lasting effects. For example, breastfeeding has been shown to protect babies against childhood cancers, lessens your little one's chances of developing type 2 diabetes, and benefits their sight (Medela, n.d.).

In addition, breastfeeding has a calming effect on your baby, which can help soothe your little one while teething or when cranky due to the flu. Actually, think of it as a miracle worker capable of pacifying even the most upset little ones.

Benefit for Moms

Not only your bundle of joy will benefit from extended breastfeeding—it lowers your risk of developing heart disease, type 2 diabetes, and various cancers (Medela, n.d.). And you'll be glad to read that your period will be missing in action for many months while you're still breastfeeding—even up to two years (Gross, 1991).

Also, are you desperate to get back your pre-pregnancy body? Then breastfeeding is your answer. Research shows that your body mass index will lower by 1% for every six months spent breastfeeding (Oddy et al., 2010).

If you consider the potential benefits, it's not surprising that a growing number of mothers choose to breastfeed for longer than what is viewed as the norm. A lot of mommies will breastfeed until their child decides it is time to stop.

Although that is an option for some mothers, not everything will have the luxury of being around their baby when it is time for their next feeding. Times have changed, and a lot of households have working moms. To these moms: your child can still benefit. The goodness lies inside the milk and doesn't depend on the child drinking straight from the source. Using a breast pump to express milk is more than adequate for your baby to continue enjoying the advantages of mother's milk.

Weaning Your Little One

If you decide to use a breast pump, you will have to wean your baby to a sippy cup or a bottle. There's no universal way to wean your little one, but if you follow a few golden rules, the transition will run much more smoothly.

As we discovered, there's no ideal time to wean your baby from your breast—it all depends on your lifestyle. If you have to go back to work, you may need to start the process earlier than you would like, and that is okay. Figuring out when exactly to start depends on your child's temperament—if you have a happy-go-lucky tot, who has no trouble handling transition, then you can begin the process at any time. However, if your baby doesn't deal with changes in a positive manner, then you may want to choose a time when things are stable in their lives. Deciding to do the jump from breast to bottle at a time when your baby is going through significant change—for example, starting daycare, moving homes, or even learning to walk—is never a good idea.

But how do you go about this change?

Your baby may actually make things easy for you by losing interest in nursing. Your little one is experiencing sensory overload at the moment—they have a lot of things to look at and sounds to pay attention to. This means they may end up pulling off the breast constantly to ease their curiosity. If you're considering weaning, then this may be your window.

On the other hand, some babies may want to be closer to their mommies more than ever at this age. Separation anxiety usually shows up at nine months, but your little one may experience it sooner. If they are extra clingy, wait a while before you start weaning—you don't want to add to their anxiety by taking away their primary source of comfort.

Here are some more tips to help you wean your tiny tot.

Give your little one extra attention. One of the main things mommy and baby miss when nursing ends is the intimacy that goes with it. You can substitute this with something that is emotionally equivalent. Add some extra snuggles to the day or extend playtime to make up for the closeness that went away with breastfeeding.

Use distractions. At times when your baby is hankering for your breast, divert her attention to a game of peek-a-boo, or something similar.

Partial Weaning

You don't have to take an all-or-nothing approach when it comes to weaning. If you're a working mom, you may want to consider partial weaning where your baby drinks from a bottle during the day when you're not available but from your breast at night when you're home.

You can pump breast milk for feedings during the day, or you can let the caregiver give your little one formula. I recommend you let your baby nurse right before you leave for the day and as soon as you get home at night to prevent engorgement. Alternatively, you can pump at work at the times your baby would generally have nursed.

Don't Forget About Mom

Things can get very uncomfortable for mommies who stop breastfeeding too quickly. Engorged breasts can be extremely painful, and you may have to express milk to alleviate some of the tenderness. When you extract milk, make sure to do just enough for comfort. If you express too much, weaning may take longer since you're still signaling your breasts to continue producing the same amount as when your baby was still nursing.

Keep an eye out for blocked duct or mastitis once you stop breastfeeding. If you have lumps in your breasts (a common occurrence for up to 10 days) and one of them is sore, you may want to contact your doctor. Give it 24 hours and if the pain hasn't gone away or you start experiencing flu-like symptoms, see your doctor as soon as possible.

If none of the lumps are tender, massage them and then express a small amount of milk to reduce the lumpiness.

Ouch! Nipple Biting

I feel your pain. I've been through it three times and can honestly say that calling a 'baby' bite isn't accurate—it's more like your nipple getting slammed in a car door! So, what do you do if you want to continue breastfeeding, but your baby is using your nipple as a chew toy? The good news is that your little one can learn to stop biting. You just have to grit your teeth and take the pain until they stop.

Understanding why babies bite is the first step to figuring out what you can do to avoid this from happening again. But before we get to the why and hows, did you know that babies can't bite while they're actively nursing? These painful nibbles actually happen between active suckling. Okay, here are the four main reasons behind your baby's bite and some tips for getting them to stop hurting mommy.

Your Baby is Teething

Teething is a painful process for your baby—their gums are sore and swollen. When your baby starts to bite during this time, the chances are that they're not in the mood to breastfeed but looking to relieve the pain. Give them a teething toy to soothe their gums—not your nipple. I also highly recommend making your tiny tot some breast milk popsicles for when they're teething. Not only will they get in the nutrients they need, but the cold will numb some of the pain.

Your Tiny Tot is Curious

Remember earlier when I said your baby is experiencing sensory overload at this age? Well, this is often the cause of biting while breastfeeding. Your little one is so distracted by what is going on around them, they quickly get bored with your breast. This will usually happen when they've had enough milk. To stop your baby from biting out of boredom, nurse in a quiet environment with little distraction.

They Want to Get Your Attention

The older your baby gets, the more attention they'll demand, and when they feel ignored, they may bite you to get noticed. To make your little one feel like all your attention is on them, keep eye contact, and engage with them while breastfeeding. Focusing on your baby at this time will also make it easier for you to see if your baby is actively nursing or if you can expect a bite any time soon. If you feel your baby draw their tongue backward, it means they're not suckling anymore. Remove them as soon as they're done to prevent a potential bite.

Your Little One Wants More Milk

Your milk supply may take a dip for various reasons, including the start of your period, some medications, birth control, and stress. When this happens, your baby may give your nipple a quick bite to get more milk to be expressed from your breast. If you're unsure about your milk supply, just keep an eye on your baby's weight—if they keep gaining at the recommended rate, then they're getting enough milk, and they may be biting for another reason.

How to Stop the Biting

Many breastfeeding experts recommend taking babies off the breast and ending the nursing session as soon as they bite. You can calmly tell your little one something such as "Don't bite mommy." After waiting a few minutes, you can attempt to nurse your baby again if they seem interested. When they release your nipple gently after feeding, you can praise them and tell them they did a good job.

This method will teach your baby that biting has a negative consequence: it removes their food source.

If your baby is clamped down and doesn't want to release their bite right away, avoid the urge to pull back—you may injure your nipple. Instead, put your finger between your little one's gums or teeth and break the suction. It will then be effortless to remove your baby from your breast. Another option is to pull your baby a little closer to your chest for just a second, forcing them to open their mouth to breathe and consequently releasing your nipple.

Some words of reassurance: biting is temporary. It is a temporary habit that your baby will quickly learn to stop when you follow the tips above.

BABY PROOFING THE HOUSE

Looking around your home and figuring out what changes you should make to keep your baby safe is an overwhelming task. If you add all the baby proofing products to the mix and new parents may quickly get lost in a long list of 'must-have' items.

Do you really need to baby proof your home? The answer is a resounding yes! But one thing you don't have to do is buy all the latest and greatest safety products—using your intuition is more than sufficient. A great place to start is getting rid of anything that could pose a risk—fireplace tools, wobbly furniture, heavy decorations, for example.

If you're not sure if a room is safe enough, count how many times you will have to tell your baby 'no.' The idea behind baby proofing your home is to create a safe space where you don't have to keep a constant eye on your tiny tot, and they don't have to be cautioned every two seconds.

Here are my top 13 baby proofing tips to give you peace of mind once your baby starts exploring their environment—even if only crawling around on the ground.

1. Check your hot-water heater settings

Babies love playing with knobs, and although your baby may not be able to walk to the bathroom and reach the heater—yet—they do spend time in the tub with it is bathtime. Before an accident happens and they turn on the hot water, make sure your hot-water heater is set to less than 120 degrees. It's something easy to do, but a lot of parents don't think of it, and their baby ends up in the emergency room with burns.

2. Keep bathrooms locked

A lot of accidents happen in bathrooms. Babies can drown in small amounts of water, so never leave your child unsupervised when in the bathroom. In addition, bathroom cabinets are filled with medication and harmful products. Since your baby is fascinated by what is packed away in closets and cupboards, the only way to stop them from exploring is to limit their access to the bathroom. You'll also prevent them from playing in the toilet if you keep the door closed and secured. I suggest you get some door knob covers to make it harder for your little one to open doors. Yes, they may not be able to walk yet, but these small humans can quickly turn into magicians, who can open doors with some effort.

3. Crib safety

Selecting the appropriate crib-rail height is essential when your baby reaches the seven-month mark. When your baby was a newborn, setting the crib at its highest wasn't a safety hazard. But now that your little one can pull themselves up, you have to lower it entirely. If you don't, your baby will be able to pull up and launch themselves out—making broken bones and a trip to the emergency room a high probability.

Let's pause for a moment. I want to share with you an interesting fact: babies are born without a fear of heights. It's only when babies get more experience navigating the world on their own that they'll start to avoid heights. They may not necessarily be afraid of heights until an experience triggers the fear. You may be asking why little ones are such daredevils who take chances on the edges of beds, couches and aren't afraid to leap out of their cribs. Isn't it safer for them if they come with a built-in fear of heights? Researchers believe this delayed fear response has a major benefit: it allows infants to explore their environment and move around without being concerned about the consequences of their actions (Dahl et al., 2013). In short, their lack of fear helps them improve movement strategies and discover how to navigate different types of surfaces. Interesting, right?

Okay, one last word on your baby's crib safety. Placing any objects in your baby's crib is a big no-no. Blankets, pillows, soft toys, even crib bumpers become more of a hazard than anything.

4. Clear out any heavy objects

Time to get down on your baby's level and look at the surroundings from their point of view. Do you see a cabinet with heavy things on it, or maybe the cabinet itself is a little wonky and needs securing? Is the television set in your baby's reach? Remember, your baby is going to use whatever they can to pull themselves up, and it is up to you to make sure nothing will topple over and fall on them. Secure large furniture items with safety straps and mount the TV to the wall instead of resting it on a cabinet or dresser.

5. Check electrical outlets

Your baby wants to poke, prod, and examine everything that's part of their world, including electric sockets. To prevent any electrocutions, buy tight-fitting electrical socket covers instead of those individual outlet covers that you just plug in. Your baby's tiny fingers may be able to pull out these individual covers, turning them into a choking hazard while leaving the electric socket open for curious fingers.

6. Secure the window blinds

I don't know what it is with toddlers, but they love to put things around their necks. For this reason, you should keep blind cords out of reach. You can replace corded window coverings with cordless options or find ways to make cords inaccessible. The best option is to replace current window treatments with something safer, but as a temporary fix, you can use wraps to keep blind cords out of your little one's reach.

7. Make a "small object tester"

Use an old toilet paper tube to help determine if an object is a choking hazard. This DIY tester is especially helpful if there are siblings in the home with toys that can be dangerous to the little one. Explain to them that any object that fits into the tube can be considered a choking hazard and should be kept away from their baby brother or sister.

8. Be careful of stairways

Safety gates are a must if you have a stairway in your house. Your little one should not be allowed to go up or down the stairs without your help. Don't wait for an accident to happen—put up a gate the minute your baby starts moving around. I recommend you fit a semi-permanent gate that is easily screwed into place. It won't fall down, and you don't have to move the whole thing when you don't need it—just keep it open.

9. Hide any chemical products

If you don't have a cabinet that is high enough to be out of your baby's reach, then lock the bottom cabinets that contain cleaning and laundry products. Laundry pods look a lot like sweets, and your baby won't think twice about popping it in their mouth.

Not only is it a choking hazard, but it will expose them to poisonous chemicals. The same goes for pills and other medications—always lock medicine cabinets and never leave any lying around where your baby can get to them.

10. Soften the corners

All babies attract sharp corners like they're magnets. Again, get down on your little one's level and see if you can spot any areas that need to be baby proofed. You can place corner guards on tables to prevent any bloody injuries should your baby lose their balance (it's going to happen) and fall. I know this isn't the most attractive option, but unless you decide to move all the tables out of the house, you're going to have to live with these baby bumpers for the next couple of years. I recommend you glue these corner guards on to make them extra secure.

11. Be careful of window falls

Use window stops to help secure windows to open no more than four inches. You get stoppers you can screw into the window frame, a more temporary option that attaches with suction, and also bars you can place across the window—they all work equally well.

12. Pack away the tablecloths

I'm sure by now you realize that your house is not going to be featured in a décor magazine any time soon. Well, not until your child is old enough to move around the house safely. You'll have to deal with corner guards, window stops, and now I'm taking away your tablecloths. Unfortunately, when your baby is learning to walk, they will use anything to help pull themselves up. They won't realize that tablecloths slip and slide until the table's contents land on their head. Instead of using tablecloths, use some placemats.

13. Create a safe play space

You won't be able to be glued to your baby's side 24/7, so give them a safe space where they can play and explore, and you don't have to worry about accidents happening. Secure the playpen so that your little one can't Houdini themselves out of it and fill it with some stimulating toys to keep them busy. You also don't want this play space to be too far from you —you should be able to see and hear your tiny tot.

OUTDOOR SAFETY

The focus is often only on the inside of the home, but the outdoors present a few hazards too—some more obvious than others. We all know that swimming pools can be dangerous but what about common objects found in the backyard?

Playing outside is meant to be fun but injuries can happen in a split second if you don't think on your feet—or well in advance to prevent any accidents, to begin with. Here are some tips to childproof your yard.

Pad the furniture: Outdoor tables have sharp corners too!

Watch the fixtures: Hoses and nozzles get very hot if they're exposed to direct sunlight so keep them in shadier areas, or better yet, put them away if not in use. Crawl around and look for any hard fixtures such as taps protruding from your home. Cover these so that your baby doesn't bump and hurt their head. Also, outdoor electrical sockets should be treated as inside ones.

Check the plants: A lot of the plants inside our homes or planted in the backyard are poisonous—some when touched, others when digested. Do some research and get rid of these.

Cover fire pits: Coals stay hot long after they've been used. You must cover any fire pits to avoid any nasty burn wounds. Although they're great additions to your yard, they're also tripping hazards, so you may want to hold off on building one until your child understands to stay away.

Secure all play structures: Play equipment should always be placed on level ground to avoid it tipping over. I suggest you check the area often as the evenness of the ground can change after heavy rain or even drought. Also, buy any play structures from reputable sources and keep things age-appropriate.

Create a soft landing: Your child is going to trip and fall many times when playing outside, especially if they're learning to walk. To take away some of the blow, add grass to the play area—it's much less painful to fall on grass than cement. Gravel should be avoided entirely as it is difficult for babies learning to walk to do so properly on it and it will also hurt a lot if there's a fall.

Watch the water: If you have a family-sized pool it should be surrounded by a fence that is locked when not in use. As for kiddies pools, empty them between use. Remember, tiny tots can drown in just a few inches of water. Furthermore, standing water poses a different type of danger when filled with bacteria and insects.

Barricade outdoor stairs: It doesn't have to be a whole stairway for stairs to be dangerous—even one or two can be a tripping hazard. If you can't remove these steps, provide a barrier so that your little one can't get up or down them.

Lock away garden equipment: Electrical yard equipment like lawnmowers and even small gardening tools like trowels and rakes can be dangerous in the hands of a toddler. Store these in an area that can be locked.

Contain your child: It is a great idea to fence your yard to keep your little one from wandering off. I suggest you add an automatic closing spring on the gate to safeguard against any forgetfulness.

Safely store BBQ and accessories. Keeping your child away from the BBQ while you're grilling is common sense, but the danger isn't limited to Sunday afternoon barbeques. You have to safely store propane tanks and make sure there aren't any hot coals your child may want to play with. Also, put away any sharp tongs or BBQ utensils.

Swimming Lessons

You may want to start infant swimming lessons as an additional safety measure, especially if you have a pool in your yard. Some parents start as early as five months, but as long as you get your baby used to the water before they develop a concept of fear, all is good. This usually happens around the eight-month mark.

Of course, your baby won't wow you by actually swimming at this young age. The goal of infant swimming lessons is to give your little one the preliminary skills and comfort with water needed to be a successful swimmer later on. The foundational knowledge and motor skills they learn will help them stay safe in and around water when they're older. As infants, they will learn to kick and paddle and this will translate into swimming in no time.

I am a big advocate for early swimming lessons—it teaches young children to roll onto their back to float when or grab onto the edge of the pool when they happen to find themselves in a dangerous situation in the water. It may only buy them a few minutes, but this can be the difference between drowning and getting rescued.

When you're looking for an aquatic facility close to you, you should focus on one that provides a safe environment for learning. It should be clean, safe, and well maintained. The water should not be treated with too many chemicals, there should be a dedicated lifeguard, and safety rules should be visible all over the facility. They should also require non-potty trained little ones to wear swim diapers.

Okay mommies, month seven went swimmingly! Your baby is entering month eight of their life. Let's see what you can expect.

MONTH EIGHT

*T*hings are getting increasingly busy in your household—baby is exploring, learning a lot, moving around constantly, and getting more sophisticated during interactions and play. If you're a stay-at-home mom, you're most likely running around trying to keep up with your little one.

Your baby should be very close to crawling if they aren't already scooting around all over the place. They're also talking up a storm with their ability to communicate expanding daily—using sounds, facial expressions, and gestures to get your attention is commonplace at this age. They're stringing together more vowel and consonant sounds and soon you'll hear those all-important words you've been waiting for since you held them the first time: mama and dada.

Since you're the most important people in your baby's life at the moment, it is no wonder that they're a little wary of people they don't know. This sudden fear of strangers doesn't mean your little one has morphed into an anti-social butterfly—it's expected at this stage of their development. It will pass; until then, give your baby space to socialize on their own terms.

Of course, your little one may want space from strangers but you can anticipate them clinging to a favorite blanket or stuffed animal. Your cutie now realizes that they can separate or be separated from you, and this understanding is both exciting and unsettling. They will become attached to a comfort object to stand in when mommy or daddy isn't close by. Let your baby bring that comfort along wherever they go; it is developmentally appropriate.

It's around this time that you're little one will start to play what I call the 'oopsie' game. Your baby's brain is starting to figure out cause and effect and object permanence. This will trigger behavior that you may find annoying but it is crucial to their development.

Let me give you an example. Your eight-month-old tiny tot is sitting in their high chair at the dinner table. They have some of their favorite foods in front of them and have a spoon in hand. But they don't eat, instead, they throw the spoon on the ground over and over again, frantically giggling when you pick it up and give it to them.

At first, you may think your baby is out to drive you crazy on purpose! But what is actually happening is them realizing, "when I drop the spoon, mommy picks it up" and "I can't see the spoon, but wait, there it is again." This game of 'oopsie' may be hard on your back and frustrate you to no end, but this routine is a sign that your baby is developing crucial memory and abstract thinking skills.

When it comes to your eight-month-old and eating, things may be getting a little strange—eating off the floor kind of strange.

BAD EATING HABITS

Your baby's dining etiquette isn't as refined as you would like it and phrases like, "don't lick the floor," "stop eating mud," and "leave the candy that fell on the sidewalk alone" will become mantras. Sorry to say, but your little one has no idea that eating things off the floor isn't considered OK, and trying to stop them from putting unsavory things in their mouth is going to be a full-time job.

But what about the three-second rule (five-second rule to some)? There's actually no scientific basis for this rule—food picks up germs as soon as it falls on the floor. The good news is that eating food off the floor inside your house won't do your little one any harm as long as it is kept fairly clean.

Your baby would already have been exposed to any germs in your house since the toys they play with will have these microorganisms on them. And, interestingly enough hard floors like tile transfer more germs than carpeted floors.

When it comes to eating food off the floor from other places, you can relax—it will strengthen your baby's immune system when they're exposed to these other germs. In fact, studies have shown that growing up in an environment that is too clean, can compromise a child's immune system, and this increases their risk of developing asthma and allergies (Bloomfield et al., 2006). This doesn't mean you should leave your baby to enjoy a buffet off the floor—there are enough germs on other surfaces to give the immune system a good workout. Clean your carpets and floor regularly, and if you're worried about germs from outside coming in, remove your shoes in the hallway.

That being said, there are some things your little one might pop into their mouth that can be harmful. Stopping these unhealthy and unsafe objects from reaching your baby's mouth will require some heroic effort!

Wet food. This is at the very top of the "extremely unhealthy" list. A day-old cookie that got wet, a pacifier left in a puddle of juice, or Sunday's sweet potato spillage left to decompose until Wednesday—soggy food or items should stay out of your baby's mouth. Bacteria multiply on wet surfaces like bunnies in a park, so don't overload your child's immune system by allowing them to eat these definite no-nos.

Food on the ground outside. There really is no three-second rule when it comes to the outdoors. Any objects that were dropped on the ground outdoors or found there should not come near your little one's mouth. Dogs and other animals walk (and leave excrement) there, so before you pop a pacifier that fell on the ground back in your baby's mouth, rinse it under water or use a wet wipe and cloth to clean it.

Lead alert. The paint used on homes built before 1978 contain lead, and this can be toxic to babies—even in tiny amounts. If you live in an older house, check all baseboards and window sills for peeling paint.

Choking hazards. Even though germs and babies can mix to some degree, bite-size dangers are a whole different story. Keep any objects that can potentially cause your baby to choke out of their reach—and mouth. Do a quick sweep of the area where your little one will be playing to make sure there aren't any coins, hard candies, Legos, buttons, and other small objects lying around. Remember the toilet paper tube test mentioned earlier? Use that to remove anything that can potentially be a choking hazard.

A toy swept under the couch, the nursery rhyme book you couldn't find yesterday, last week's teething biscuit—if it's on the floor, it will most likely find its way into your little one's mouth. While you shouldn't cheer your baby one when they eat off the floor, you don't have to panic—some good does come from being exposed to germs.

GENITAL DISCOVERY

It's at this point in the book where I want to tell you to get out of your own head. Your baby will, anytime from now, start to discover their genitals. Now, we tend to look at this self-exploration from an adult perspective and see it as something sexual—it's not. Your baby has no life experience, their brain is still developing, their nervous system is still immature, and they don't have a lot of social awareness—of course, some of the things they do will make no sense to us.

The first thing I want you to know is that your little one's touching of their genitals isn't masturbation—it's exploration. There is no sexual intent or emotion behind this act. Yes, it feels good and in some cases gives them comfort, but that's about as far as it goes.

Babies start playing with their private parts as early as five-months-old. They're eager to learn and explore their environment—and themselves. Think about it; your baby constantly plays with their hands and feet, and yet it doesn't get the same reaction as when they touch their genitals. Yes, they may linger a little longer in this area because it feels good, but to them, it's ultimately just another way of learning about their bodies.

I know you're wondering if you should leave them or attempt to do something about it. Won't it lead to sexual perversion if you let them be? Firstly, how you react to this type of behavior should depend on where you are. Some things are okay to do in public, others are not, and this is something you'll have to teach your kid as they grow up.

But I'm getting ahead of myself, let's look at what you should and shouldn't do.

Don't shame or scold your child. Any negative response from you may make the behavior more tempting. But that's not the worst of it, you may make them feel ashamed of their body and the feelings they have if you make a fuss. I recommend you ignore the behavior entirely if you're in the privacy of your own home.

When out in public, try to distract your child with a hands-on activity like drawing or building blocks. If they're not interested in diverting their attention away from their genitals, look away. Other toddlers won't even notice and your friends and family will understand. If they don't agree with how you're handling the situation, you can attempt to educate them or remove yourself and your baby from their company to avoid them shaming your little one.

Explain to your tiny tot the difference between public and private areas. If they start touching themselves when you're out in public, calmly and quietly tell them that it's not okay to do it in public where other people can see them. Try to distract them and remember to praise them when they stop touching their private parts in public.

Check if your little one wants to go to the bathroom. You may have noticed that many toddlers hold their genitals when they need to go pee. Before assuming your baby is touching themselves, ask them if they want to go to the toilet.

The only time you have to worry about this behavior is if your child becomes obsessed with their 'touchy' habit. Talk to your pediatrician when this happens—underlying stress may be driving them to find comfort in this way.

Erections

Yes, babies do get erections—they even have them while still in the womb! Again, this is not a sexual response but a normal reaction to touch. Remember, the penis is a sensitive organ and your baby may get a reaction when you're washing their penis or when a diaper rubs against it. Then again, it may happen at random times also.

As your little one grows and becomes more mobile, they will start to explore their bodies as discussed above. They may even try to make their penis erect. So you may see your tiny tot have frequent erections —but they won't lead to ejaculation. It's only around the age of 11 when your boy goes into puberty that they'll be able to ejaculate.

I know it may be a bit shocking at first, but don't worry. Instead, take it as a sign that everything is in good working order down there. This exploration forms part of growing up. When they get older, you'll just have to help manage the touching and rubbing so that it's not embarrassing for them, you, or other people.

CROOKED TEETH

Don't plan a trip to the orthodontist just yet—it's actually quite common for your little one's first teeth to be crooked. The front teeth are especially prone to unevenness. I know you're concerned but you really don't have to worry about your baby's dental health.

But doesn't crooked baby teeth mean that they'll have permanent crooked teeth later? There's no way to predict how your child's adult teeth will look based on the appearance of the baby teeth. Your little one will only have a full set of pearly whites around two and a half years of age. They also won't come out in perfect proportion.

What causes crooked teeth to begin with? The most significant factor is genetics. If your baby inherited a small jaw from you and large teeth from their dad, then the likelihood of overcrowding in the mouth is present.

Babies who suckle on their thumb may also be the reason behind the misalignment of the teeth due to the pressure on both the upper and lower teeth. It's less common for extra teeth to cause overcrowding in the mouth.

Is there something you can do when you notice your baby's teeth coming in crooked?

You don't have much control over your baby's smile. The best you can do is to seek the opinion of a trusted orthodontist. Thanks to modern orthodontic practices, you don't need to wait until their adult teeth have emerged to address any issues. Your baby's dentist will be able to investigate any abnormalities and suggest the best course of action.

Children can be fitted with a removable retainer-like device from a relatively young age. This gadget will help the development of the arches of the mouth while providing a better environment for emerging teeth.

I know some parents are reluctant to intervene at such a young age, but consider that being proactive will reduce the intricacy of future treatments. But your orthodontist is the best person to guide you in this regard.

IS YOUR BABY A LEFTY OR A RIGHTY?

Your baby's dominant hand was determined long before they entered this world—it's written into your cutie's DNA. Research shows that genetic differences appear in the spinal cord that will impact if your baby will be right or left-handed even before the brain and spinal cord are linked (Ocklenburg et al., 2017).

This doesn't mean your doctor will be able to tell you whether your little one will be a lefty or a righty based on their behavior in the womb. It's just a fun guessing game to play—much like wondering if your baby will have blue or brown eyes. But then again, an older study found that the preferred thumb babies suck in the womb may indicate their dominant hand (Hepper, Wells & Lynch, 2005). Researchers report that 90% of babies who sucked their right thumb ended up being right-handed. Add to that the fact that 90% of the population is right-handed and you'll even be able to make quite an accurate 'guestimate' of your baby's dominant hand.

Also, when your little one reaches for toys, you'll notice them using their left and right hand interchangeably. This is normal. Where some children may have a clear preference by their first birthday, others can take up to the age of three or four to make up their mind. Hand dominance evolves with your baby's fine-motor skills, and until those skills are fully developed, both hands will get equal playtime.

But does it matter? Not really. While some people want to believe that being a southpaw gives them some advantage, there is no proof that it does. The only real 'specialness' connected to being left-handed is the fact that only 10 to 12 percent of people are born as lefties. So, if you have a left-handed child, you have a left-handed child and not some genius as some parents believe.

MONTH NINE

*Y*ou're three months away from your baby's first birthday! How does it feel to know that you've raised a tiny little human—most likely with little to no incident or major accidents?

At month nine, your baby's cute "goo-goo-gaga" is possibly real life words. If you did hear your baby's cute little voice say 'mamma' yet, this may be your month! In addition, most babies will be able to say ball, bye-bye, and other words they heard often. If your baby hasn't uttered something understandable yet, no need to worry, they will in time.

It's time to get your baby some push and riding toys if you haven't already. Also, look for playthings that will promote physical development. Of course, you're a great source of entertainment and make a great playmate, so get down on your knees and crawl around with your tiny tot. I used to stack pillows and encourage my baby to follow me as I went over it. Tunnels to crawl through, large balls to roll, musical toys, and some starter art supplies will make great additions to a nine-month-old's toy box.

Since their brain is getting more sophisticated, their old rattles and teethers "are so yesterday, mom." Time for your little one to move on to the bigger-kid stuff where they can play with switches and levers, push buttons, grab knobs—anything that they can manipulate and master will provide hours of fun.

Your baby will also now be able to respond to one-step commands combined with gestures. For example, asking your little one to give you the toy while your hand is open and out may see them doing just that! They'll also be able to indicate if they want something and it won't just be through crying.

You will also have to up your discipline at this time since your tiny tot can understand 'no' and the overall body language and facial expressions that go with the word. Don't be afraid to reprimand your baby when they're doing something that could cause them harm. Discipline is one of the hard parts of parenting, so get an early start. Also check out some books on positive parenting to avoid your house turning into a warzone filled with angry screams as your little one grows older.

YOUR NINE-MONTH-OLD AND FOOD

Your infant is more confident when it comes to eating so you can offer them more lumpy and finger foods. Serving them food that they don't have to eat with a spoon will encourage self-feeding and more importantly, develop their hand and eye coordination.

When it comes to the nutrients your baby needs, think of what you need: five servings of fruit and vegetables each day even though their serving sizes are significantly less than what you'd consume. And yes, they also need protein in their diet, but it's the fruit and veggies that are the toughest to work into a diet, especially a variety and not just, say, pumpkin. I always tell my clients to think of feeding their little ones the rainbow.

- Green: Broccoli, peas, spinach, green beans, asparagus, zucchini
- Orange: Cantaloupe, sweet potatoes, peaches
- Yellow: Squash, bananas
- Red: Tomatoes, red peppers

What you don't want to do is give them a cup of juice as a fruit serving. It's not as nutritious as you think—you're basically giving your baby a sugary syrup to drink. You also don't want the juice to replace breast milk or formula or your little one won't get their protein needs met. I recommend you always dilute the juice when you do give it to your tiny tot as a special treat.

I know you're probably stumped when it comes to what foods to give your baby—I mean, you don't want to serve them the same thing day in and day out. Here are some ideas of what you can give your little one to keep things interesting.

Breakfast

- Oatmeal: Use unsweetened oats and mix it with breast milk, formula, or water. You can stir in some banana or steamed apples or pears to sweeten the oatmeal and add some variety.

- Pancakes/waffles: Use whole-grain mix if you can and mix in some wheat germ for some extra health benefits. Top with pureed fruit instead of sugary, non-nutritious bottled syrup.
- Eggs: Scramble some eggs with a tablespoon of cottage cheese. You can even make your little one a tiny omelet filled with softened veggies.

Lunch

- Grilled cheese: Use whole-wheat bread with the crusts removed. You can add a little butter but don't overdo it. Once the cheese is melted, let it cool and cut into small bites before giving it to your baby.
- Yogurt: Your baby's taste buds hopefully haven't tasted flavored and sweetened yogurt yet, so stick to the unsweetened kind for as long as you can. You can sweeten the deal by adding some jarred or home-

steamed fruit. To amp up the taste, combine more than one fruit.

- Peanut butter sandwich: The consistency of peanut butter makes it a choking hazard, so use very little peanut butter and spread it thinly. Use soft bread with the crusts cut off. If you're tired of serving your little one peanut butter, use some avocado, hummus, or cream cheese instead.

- Soup: Broiled veggies and noodle soup served lukewarm and only a little at a time will keep your baby hydrated too. You can add some mashed beans or shredded cheese.

- Macaroni and cheese: Cook noodles until soft and add some shredded cheese. You can stir in some pureed vegetables for a nutrient boost.

Dinner

- Baked potato: Remove the skin and mash the potato in butter, cheese, and some pureed veggies. You can add some beans to the mix too.

- Pasta/couscous: Blitz it in a mini food processor with some homemade tomato sauce. If you're forced to use store-bought sauce, don't add any extra seasoning. Cooked veggies or shredded meats will add that something extra your baby deserves.

- Lasagna: If lasagna is on the menu for the family tonight, don't think the baby has to eat something else. As long as it is not overly spiced, you can put some of your lasagna in a food processor and let your baby enjoy the same meal as you and your family—even if it is a little mushed. The same goes for any other family dinners that don't contain potential allergens or choking hazards. And remember, your baby is now nine months old so food doesn't need to be perfectly smooth anymore.

You have the ability to set a healthy foundation for your child's eating habits. Make their meals healthy and tasty, and your baby will be well on their way to a lifetime of healthy food choices.

Cow's Milk

A lot of parents can't wait to transition their babies to cow's milk—it's cheaper and more convenient. But is it safe? A while ago, it was considered safe to start giving babies cow's milk at six months, then the age got pushed up to nine months, and now it is recommended that you wait until they are one year old (Leung & Sauve, 2003). This is due to a few reasons.

- Starting cow's milk too early can increase your baby's chance of food allergies and worse, diabetes (Gottlieb, 2000).
- Drinking cow's milk before one year of age can lead to anemia since formula and breast

milk contain more nutrients your baby needs to grow.

- Infants cannot digest cow's milk before they turn one.
- Cow's milk contains a lot of protein and minerals which may stress your young baby's kidneys.
- Cow's milk doesn't contain healthy fats.

Loss of Interest in Nursing

Earlier, you read that your baby's curious nature may make it difficult to keep them latched onto your breast. At this age (and earlier), it is very easy for them to become distracted. At the nine-month mark, they may refuse your breast entirely or appear to be self-weaning. You have two options when this happens: wean your baby or try to get them to stop the nursing strike.

One way to differentiate between self-weaning and a nursing strike is to look at how fast it happens. Babies who are ready to wean will do so over a period of weeks or months, but when your baby suddenly refuses your breast, it's probably a nursing strike.

This can be a very upsetting experience for mommies who want to continue breastfeeding until later in their child's life. In the same breath, it's not a nice thing for your baby to go through either. The good news is that it's almost always temporary and your little one will be back on your breast in two to four days.

Here are some of the more common triggers of breast rejection.

- You're wearing a new deodorant, perfume, body lotion, or you changed your soap. In other words, you smell 'different' to your little one.
- You've been under stress.
- Your baby is suffering from an ear infection, thrust, a stuffy nose, or a cut in the mouth that makes nursing painful.
- Your little one has sore gums from teething.
- You changed your nursing routine.
- You had a negative reaction when your baby bit you and this left them frightened.
- You're not making enough milk due to being pregnant, ovulating, or pumping less

frequently. Medication can also impact your supply.

- Your milk sprays fast and hard and your baby can't control it. This is called strong or overactive letdown and it will cause your baby to refuse your breast.

I know you're feeling frustrated and upset. You may even feel like your baby is rejecting you but that is not the case at all. With a little patience and persistence, you will get your little one to nurse from your breast again in no time.

If you believe that illness or injury lies behind your baby's strike, get medical attention. I also recommend spending extra time with your little one—skin-to-skin contact and extra cuddles will help your baby to reconnect with you and re-establish closeness.

Here are some other time-tested tips to help overcome a nursing strike.

- **Don't stress about it.** Easier said than done, I know. But your baby will pick up on your stress. So, set the mood: play some relaxing music, lower the lights, and have as much skin contact as possible while your baby is nursing.

- **Give your baby your breast while they're asleep, just waking up, or very drowsy.** In these states, we have a more primitive mindset, and since breastfeeding is all about survival for babies, they may latch on to your breast like in the old days at this time.

- **Change nursing positions** until you find one your little one likes.

- **Use a sling or cloth to carry your baby around.** Nursing while in motion has a higher success rate.

- **Give your little one extra attention** and skin-to-skin contact.

- **Lay in bed topless during playtime** without any pressure to nurse. Your baby may just take this as an open invitation to nurse.

- **Breastfeed your baby in a quiet and dark room** that is free of distractions.

- **Get your milk flowing before**

offering your little one the breast.
This immediate reward may get them to
latch on for longer.

- **Let your baby sleep with you**, giving
them easy access to your breast while
sleeping.

While you're working patiently to persuade your
little one to start breastfeeding again, you have to
make sure they get enough milk to sustain them and
to keep your milk supply going. Use a cup, spoon,
syringe, or eyedropper to feed your baby while you
work on getting them back on the breast. You can use
a baby bottle if you're familiar with paced bottle
feeding—tilting the bottle too much or using fast-flow
nipples may confuse your baby more and prolong the
nursing strike.

As for mommy, you have to extract your milk to avoid
engorgement. I suggest you use hand expression or a
pump at the times your little would normally nurse.
This will keep your milk supply going while
protecting you from potentially clogged ducts, or
worse yet, mastitis.

If the strike doesn't end in a few days, it may signal the end of your breastfeeding journey. Don't feel sad, instead, think of the gift you've given your child the last couple of months. There's no doubt that this will be an emotional time, especially if you planned on nursing for longer, but take care of yourself. This is just another step in your journey as a mother.

NO PEARLY WHITES...YET

There is no set age for your baby to get their first tooth. Yes, it is true that the first tooth usually appears around six months, but this can vary enormously. Some newborns may enter the world with a tooth, while others will be captured with a gummy smile on their first birthday photos.

If your baby doesn't have any teeth at nine months, don't worry, they're just taking their time. There's also a chance that this late teething runs in the family —either you or your baby's dad were also late bloomers when it came to cutting teeth.

Here's a teething chart explaining when you can expect your baby's teeth to pop up. Of course, if your baby is a late bloomer, you may want to add a month or two (or three) to the projections.

Upper row

Show up

Fall out

Central incisor

8-12 months

6-7 years

Lateral incisor

9-13 months

7-8 years

Canine (cuspid)

16-22 months

10-12 years

First molar

13-19 months

9-11 years

Second molar

25-33 months

10-12 years

Lower row

Show up

Fall out

Second molar

23-31 months

10-12 years

First molar

14-18 months

9-11 years

Canine (cuspid)

17-23 months

9-12 years

Lateral incisor

10-16 months

7-8 years

Central incisor

6-10 months

6-7 years

Let's look at three other possible reasons why your baby doesn't have a tooth yet.

1. Poor nutrition

If your little one is not getting enough nutrition from breast milk or formula, then it will lead to delayed teething. Your baby needs calcium for the development of their teeth and bones and breast milk and formula are great sources of this vital mineral.

2. Hypothyroidism and hypopituitarism

When the thyroid glands don't produce enough thyroid hormone for your little one's body to function normally, it is called hypothyroidism. This lack of thyroid hormone affects heart rate, metabolism, and body temperature. If your baby suffers from an underactive thyroid, they will fall behind on several milestones, including walking, teething, and talking. Hypopituitarism is when there is too little of one or more of the hormones produced by the pituitary gland. This can cause several diseases and conditions linked with hormone deficiencies, including obesity, high cholesterol, and it will affect the time it takes your baby's body to make and push out teeth.

3. Medical disorders

Certain medical conditions and disorders can also cause delayed teething. Down's Syndrome is one example. It can also be caused by a physical obstruction in the gums or jaw bone which prevents the tooth from erupting.

WALKING

Has your baby started moving around on two legs? If they haven't yet, there is a possibility that you will soon see them awkwardly walking toward you with a huge grin on their face. But to understand if your little one is close to walking independently, you have to understand the stages of walking. Here's a quick timeline of the developmental milestones babies need to master before walking.

Sitting up: Your baby will figure out how to use the muscles in their body to stay upright at around six months old.

Pulling to a stand: This can happen anytime from seven months—earlier if your baby is eager to get moving around. But your little one will need a lot of strength in their legs to pull off this move—70% of their body mass is from the hips on up, so lifting their torso is no easy feat.

Cruising: As with any milestones, age varies for cruising. This usually happens shortly after your baby gets the hang of pulling themselves up to stand. Once they figure out that they can make their way around the room using furniture, they'll be cruising up and down non-stop.

Walking: The final piece of the puzzle can fall in place from nine months but it can take some babies up to 18 months to put one foot in front of the other without mommy or daddy's help.

Once your baby gets going, the next challenge will be to figure out how to stop! You'll notice your baby's steps becoming faster and more forceful as they go. They haven't yet made the link between stopping with one foot and bringing the other foot forward to meet it. This means the only way they know how to stop walking is to fall. It's like a dance: step, step, fall.

You should also keep in mind that babies alternate between crawling and walking. Since they're only now starting to walk, they may drop into a crawl if they see something that requires immediate attention. As they get more confident in walking, they won't zoom across the floor on all fours anymore but may attempt a run.

Help Your Baby Take Their First Steps

There are a million different ways you can help your little one. Some parents hold their baby's hands while they walk, others buy walkers and jumpers to encourage their tiny tots to walk. If you ask me, all you need is patience and restraint—both very difficult.

Here are my top tips for encouraging your baby to start walking independently.

- Let your baby do it at their own pace. Trust that they'll know when they're ready to take the next step—literally. If you attempt to push your little one into something they're not ready for, it will do more harm than good.
- Don't use baby walkers. The safety risks of

using baby walkers combined with the lack of benefits doesn't make it worth your money. In fact, research shows that baby walkers may slow the development of your child's walking skills (Badihian, Adihian & Yaghini, 2017).

- Give your baby time to develop naturally. There's no jumping milestones—each one builds upon the previous one. If your baby hasn't learned to sit, they won't be able to walk, and your tiny tot can't sit if they haven't mastered rolling over. Each physical milestone builds muscle strength and stability. If you continuously try to help your child by propping them up, walking them, etc., you are slowing down their development—not speeding it up. There are transitional postures in between each milestone where they learn how to move from one skill to another. Although these postures may look funny to you—for example, one leg folded under their bum and the other one bent at the knee as if they can't decide if they want to sit or stand—try not to interfere.

- Baby proof the house. We covered this in

depth earlier in the book. If your baby has a safe place to move around in, they're more likely to walk on their own.

Flat Feet

Up to 44% of infants and young children have a flattening of the arch when they stand or wal

k (Pfeiffer et al., 2006). The height of the arch of the foot will increase as your tiny tot grows older. Flat foot only becomes a problem when it persists or suddenly occurs in older children. Flat feet can be painful during weight-bearing activities. If your baby complains of any symptoms associated with flat feet, get medical advice; if there isn't any pain or discomfort, then treatment isn't needed.

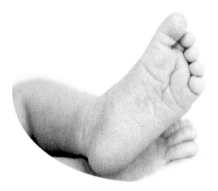

MONTH TEN

*Y*our baby is on a seek and destroy mission! Since they can move around more independently, they may seem hell-bent on getting into trouble. There truly is no surface too high or hole too deep for your ten-month-old. You will have to watch your baby like a hawk more than ever before. But that's not a bad thing— they're sure to get up to some interesting and funny things that will keep you entertained.

With so much discovering to do, there won't be time for eating or anything else at this age. They have a singular focus: explore the world. I wouldn't worry too much about their declining eating habits if I were you; the older your baby gets, the more their appetite will decrease.

Your little energizer bunny may also turn into a picky eater, but it's about more than the taste of specific foods—they're trying to assert their independence. Luckily there are plenty of tricks you can try to get choosy customers to cave—check the section, Your Solid Food Questions Answered in Chapter One.

One thing I want you to pay particular attention to from now on is praising your baby. I know you probably already do it dozens of times a day and at times you may feel you're making a fuss over nothing. Believe me, you're not. This praise builds your little one's self-esteem and makes them want to try and try again—it makes them believe in themselves. So, set your cutie up for success; give them age-appropriate toys they can accomplish with ease. But in the same breath, challenge your baby. Put objects far enough so that they need to exert some effort to get them. Then leave them to try on their own and only offer help when they get too frustrated.

Praise is more valuable when your child had to work for something than just an empty "good job." Also make an effort to use specific words of applause. Say, "Wow, you're really trying hard to get the ball," to praise your baby's effort and when they succeed, compliment them in detail. For example, instead of just saying "Good job," be more specific and acclaim, "You did it! You pushed the red block into the right hole!" This shows your baby that you're paying attention to what they're doing and not just saying generic words.

SELF-SOOTHING BEHAVIORS

Your baby is now older and self-soothing isn't limited to thumb-sucking or cuddling their favorite toy anymore. Toddlers are peculiar little beings who often have coping mechanisms that leave mommy and daddy scratching their heads in wonder. At times you won't be able to stop yourself from asking, "Is my child normal?"

I want to discuss two self-soothing behaviors that may be of concern to you, especially when you see them for the first time.

Head Banging

When your baby is in their crib, you may notice them rocking on all fours or banging and rolling their heads until they fall asleep. This behavior is common at bedtime or during the night, but I know it can be unsettling when you first see them do it.

The reason behind the body-rocking and head movements is the rhythm—it comforts and soothes them. Your little one may:

- Get on all fours and rock their body back and forth while hitting their head on the edges of the crib.
- Sit in bed, rocking back and forth, while banging their heads back against the wall or headboard.
- Lie on their tummy and bang their head into the pillow.
- Lie on their back and roll their head or body from side to side.
- Make noises while they're rocking.

As with other self-soothing behaviors, it is nothing to worry about if your baby is in good health and thriving in all other ways. The body-rocking and head-rolling and banging will eventually go away.

Here are some tips that may help prevent this behavior:

1. Don't put your child in bed too early. If they are spending a lot of time in bed before falling asleep, head-banging or body-rocking is likely to happen.
2. Don't pay attention to the behavior. If your child sees they're getting attention or that this behavior causes you to go into their room (even to tell them to stop), they'll do it more often.
3. Move the crib or bed away from the wall or other hard surfaces.

If you're worried because this behavior happens frequently, talk with your child's doctor. If your little one rocks, rolls, and bangs their head, and also snores, then their doctor may want to check for issues that are disturbing their sleep.

Hair Twirling

When your baby is stressed, bored, or getting ready to fall asleep, they may twirl their hair. Children who are prone to anxiety also find release in hair twirling. This self-comforting behavior is completely normal and will likely stop around age three or four.

However, if the hair twirling is causing hair loss or has a negative impact on your child's in other areas, there are some things you can try to help curb the behavior.

- Don't draw too much attention to their hair twirling.
- Help your little one find other ways to release pent-up energy or anxiety. Physical activities work best, so add some dancing, running, and jumping to playtime.
- Try to figure out what is causing your baby stress. Are you arguing with your spouse, is there a new baby in the house, is your little one weaning from breast to bottle? Any significant changes may trigger your child's hair twirling.
- Find a replacement for the behavior. Give your baby a soft blanket or a new stuffed animal to help them self-soothe. A doll with long hair may even be a better option—then they can twirl her hair and not their own.
- Take your baby for a haircut. If their hair is

short, it may be less tempting or more difficult for them to twirl.

The bottom line is toddlers are full of little idiosyncrasies. It forms part of what makes them so quirky and lovable. And you can't deny that it adds some comedy to your day!

NEGATIVE BEHAVIOR

For all the eccentric harmless behaviors your little one has, there are equally as many negative actions.

To put an end to these, you will have to take a firm no-nonsense approach.

Here are the top two things your ten-month-old baby may do that you need to put a stop to.

Biting

Why do children bite? Well, for several reasons, but most of them aren't malicious in nature.

They're in pain. Your little one may be teething and they're biting to make their swollen and tender gums feel a little better. They're frustrated. Young children don't always know how to express what they're feeling by using words. Instead, they'll bite or hit to assert themselves. It's their way of saying they're unhappy, they want their toy back, or want to be left alone.

They're exploring. Babies don't just use their hands to investigate their surroundings; they use their mouths too. Do you remember how everything your little one picks up goes into their mouth? Biting is not different—they're not yet capable of stopping themselves from biting something they find interesting.

They're looking for a reaction. Their exploration is not just limited to the environment; they want to explore reactions too. So, they will bite to hear the shock and surprise in someone's voice. Unfortunately, they don't yet realize that the reaction is mostly due to the pain experienced by the person. They want attention. Biting is one of the bad behaviors toddlers and older kids use to get attention—even it is the negative kind. When your little one feels ignored, they'll bite to get noticed; it doesn't matter that it comes in the form of discipline.

Breath-Holding

When your little one is especially upset, they may intentionally hold their breath until they're bright red in the face. This behavior can happen when your tiny tot is angry, scared, startled, or just bothered in general. Some babies may hold their breath until they faint. If this happens to your little one, then it's best to discuss your child's severe breath-holding with their doctor.

If it's not that serious, you can view breath-holding as a form of a temper tantrum. During breath-holding, your child may:

- Cry uncontrollably, followed by silence while they hold their breath.
- Open their mouth without making a sound.
- Turn red in the face.

In extreme breath-holding spells, your baby may experience these additional steps:

- Turn blue or grey.
- Fall over with a limp or stiff body.
- Their body may make jerking motions.
- Faint for one or two minutes.

When your child wakes up, they may be confused and sleepy.

Usually, breath-holding is harmless behavior. Yes, it's very scary from a parent's point of view, but stay calm and stay consistent in your message that holding their breath is not the best way to communicate their unhappiness.

MONTH ELEVEN

our baby won't be a baby for much longer! They're getting more independent as the days roll by and some of their behaviors are only a small taste of what lies ahead in the toddler years.

At this age, your little one is having the time of their life as they explore and babble their way to their first birthday. They came such a long way from their early baby days, haven't they? Gone are the days when your baby couldn't hold up their own head—now they're cruising around without a care in the world. Besides their ability to walk, they'll also be able to clap hands, raise their arms as a signal for you to pick them up, drink from a cup, pick up objects with the tips of their thumb and forefinger, and wave bye-bye. How awesome is that?

Can you believe that your baby weighed around 10 pounds at the one-month mark and now they can weigh up to 27 pounds! Don't even get me started on how much they have stretched.

Your eleven-month-old bundle of joy is also learning to take care of themselves at the moment. You may not even have noticed! For example, your baby may push their fists through the sleeves when you dress them, or they stretch their legs out when it is time to put on pants. I'm sure you also realized that your baby can swig milk from a cup and has become more adept at feeding (and bib, hair, lap, and the floor.)

You may also have a little adventurer on your hands —one who finds climbing exhilarating. They'll climb over the crib railing or attempt to scale kitchen counters. If your tiny tot is a little monkey, you'll have to move things around to limit their access to high places. Move chairs far enough away from tables and countertops to prevent your baby from climbing high enough to fall and hurt themselves.

Okay, let's move on to the more serious stuff you'll have to pay attention to in the month before your baby turns one-year-old.

SNACKING

You want your child to grow up with healthy snacking habits. Giving your 11-month-old the freedom to experiment with healthy snack foods will establish the foundation for your child's future dietary habits. It also boosts their independence and gives their growing bodies a boost of nutrition.

At this age, snacks will start to form an essential part of your little one's diet, especially since they're so active and can do with the extra energy during mealtimes.

But before you reach for convenience foods such as crackers, sweets, and chips, keep in mind that these foods are high in salt which can damage your baby's kidneys. Processed and packaged food also contain a lot of sugar and hidden trans fats—both linked with various diseases. Overall, it is best to avoid sugary snacks as they may turn your child into a picky eater, will damage their teeth, and can cause childhood obesity.

Fruit and veggies come out top when it comes to snack foods—they're packed full of essential vitamins and minerals. Giving your little one fruits or vegetables as snacks will also make it easier for you to meet the five-a-day dietary requirement. However, if you're bored with fruits and veggies, your tiny tot probably is too. If that's the case, you can give them yogurt, rice cakes with cream cheese, crackers with hummus, or sugar-free cereal. The options are truly endless and I will give you some more snack ideas further down.

If it's convenience you're after, then feel free to take a stroll down the baby food aisle in the supermarket. You'll find a variety of tasty treats but will have to play ingredient detective to make sure you're selecting something healthy that is not filled with preservatives, hidden sugars, bad fats, and excess calories. A lot of packaged snack foods will claim to be healthy for kids but on closer inspection, you'll see they contain high percentages of sodium, sugar and refined carbohydrates. If you give your child unhealthy snacks (the sugary and carb-high kind), you may set up a lifelong preference for these types of foods.

Also, although snacking is important, you shouldn't overdo it. Although your little one will want to graze the whole day, you don't want to spoil their appetite for the bigger meals. I recommend you give them two snacks only; one mid-morning and the other mid-afternoon. Most importantly, keep it healthy.

Giving your baby a healthy snack twice a day will help ensure they're:

- *Exposed to a varied diet.* You'll have two extra opportunities a day to offer new and different foods. If your child gets used to eating a variety of foods, they'll develop a taste and desire for a diverse and healthy diet that will stick with them into adulthood.
- *Eating enough macronutrients and micronutrients.* Your tiny tot needs to consume sufficient amounts of protein, carbohydrates, and fat, as well as calcium, iron, vitamin D, and other nutrients to fuel their rapid growth.
- *Consuming enough calories.* Babies can't handle big meals in one sitting—their

stomachs are small and fill up quickly. So to
make sure they eat enough calories, they
need to eat multiple times during the day.

- *Learning correct eating behavior.* Snack
  time can be used as an opportunity to teach
  healthy eating habits, as well as help
  develop their social skills.

One thing you have to watch out for is dropping milk
feeds. Although the amount of milk your baby needs
is decreasing, they should still get 10 oz of breastmilk
or formula per day at this age. You will also have to
find other ways to keep your energizer bunny
hydrated during their adventures since they're
drinking less milk than before. Avoid any sugary and
fizzy drinks, and if you give your baby fruit juice,
dilute one part juice to ten parts water. Still, milk
and water are the healthiest options.

Healthy Snack Ideas

To prevent you from visiting the baby aisle in the supermarket, stock your home with their favorite healthy snacks. When you plan a day out, don't forget to pack snacks so that you don't end up buying the processed kind. Here are some of my favorite snack ideas—and all three of my children agree.

- Banana, apples, pears, oranges, mango, watermelon, honeydew, and other soft, fresh fruit that can be cut into bite-size pieces.
- Plain yogurt with homemade steamed fruit added in for natural sweetness.
- Cottage cheese and berries.
- Baby carrots, string beans, sugar snap peas, green beans, broccoli, and other veggies your baby can hold in their hand and dip into some hummus or homemade dip.
- Cucumber spears.
- Avocado.
- Chickpeas, low-sodium kidney or black beans.
- Whole-grain cereal without added sugar.

- String cheese or cheese cut into cubes.
- Cubes of tofu.
- Whole-grain crackers with cheese.
- Whole-grain bread with peanut butter.
- Kale chips.
- Beetroot chips.
- Hard-boiled eggs.

I'm sure you can think of even more snack-friendly foods to add to the list. The options are endless and there's no reason for you to buy processed and packaged snack foods for your growing baby.

NAPPING

Your baby's sleeping needs at 11 months are pretty similar to the previous two months. They're likely clocking 14 hours of sleep a day, but anything between 12 to 16 hours is considered normal. Your little one's sleeping schedule is probably fairly predictable with them waking up early in the morning, a morning and afternoon nap, and bedtime at 7 or 8 pm.

You're probably also pretty relieved that your little rascal is sleeping through the night without needing a feeding.

When it comes to nap time, you want to aim to put your baby down two times a day for two to two and a half hours in total. Some babies will nap only once a day but in general, you should plan for two naps.

Although baby naps are a restful time for you and your tiny tot, it's not always an easy task to get them to sleep during the day. Unluckily, babies who don't take naps become cranky little creatures you can't control but what's worse is that they'll refuse to sleep at bedtime because they're overtired. When you do get them to sleep, their night will be restless as they struggle to settle. As you can see, naps ironically form an essential part of a good night's sleep.

A happy, well-rested baby equals a happy and well-rested mommy, so here are some tips to get your baby to stop fighting against daytime naps.

Set the mood. Close the curtains, turn off the radio and TV, and create a quiet and dark environment to help encourage your baby to take a nap.

Start a nap routine. Just as you have a bedtime routine, set up one for daytime naps. Sing a soft lullaby, give them a massage, or swaddle them tightly. These activities will, in time, signal that it is time to rest.

Be consistent. It's more likely that your baby will happily go for a snooze when they're used to doing it at the same time each day and for the same length of time. Their body will also after a while instinctively know that it is time for a nap. Of course there will be days where you can't stick to the schedule, but don't worry, it won't wipe out all your progress.

In the beginning, nap times are hardly ever stress-free but helping your baby get enough daytime sleep is essential. On the days where you find it more challenging than others, don't feel bad, it happens to the best of us. Your only focus should be to keep their nap routine consistent—they'll get the memo at one point or another.

TOOTH INJURIES

Walking is dangerous business, especially when you're still finding your feet. Most dental injuries happen from falls but there are other reasons why you may have to visit the dentist earlier than you expected.

The last thing you imagine happening when your baby's first teeth come in is that they'll damage or lose one, or that a cavity will spoil one of their pearly whites so early on. Here are some tips to deal with common tooth injuries and other issues.

K.O. Tooth

Close to a third of all toddlers will experience some kind of tooth-related trauma. This usually happens between 18 and 40 months but your 11-month-old baby is not clear of danger—falls are part of learning to walk.

If your child knocks out a tooth, do the following:

Stop the bleeding. Apply firm pressure to the hole. If the bleeding doesn't stop after 10 minutes, take your child to the emergency room.

Give your baby something to relieve the pain. It's always good to keep baby-safe pain medication in the house. If you're not sure what medicine is safe to give to your little one, check with your doctor and stock up on what they recommend.

Call the dentist. Your baby's dentist will know what to do when a tooth has been knocked out. For baby teeth, the dentist may feel it is better not to re-implant the tooth. The procedure may affect the permanent tooth.

Keep the tooth moist. Don't touch the root of the tooth—handle it at the top or crown side. You can drop the tooth in milk in case your dentist decides it is worthwhile to re-implant it after all. When your child is older and has permanent teeth, you may want to put the tooth back in the socket and have your child bite down. As you can imagine, this won't work for your still tiny baby.

Keep calm. Your child will most probably not feel too good when they knock out a tooth. The blood makes things look worse than they are and it won't be surprising if your child gets scared—not to mention the pain they're experiencing at that moment. Since your child is probably in a panic, you need to stay calm and do your best to soothe your baby.

Partial Break, Chip, or Crack

Your baby's first teeth are a lot more unstable than your teeth. They're much easier to damage since the crown is longer than the root, making partial breaks, chips, or cracks a high likelihood.

In some instances, you will have to get your baby to a dentist right away, in others, a next day visit will do. Your baby's tooth injury is a dental emergency when:

- The tooth is only partly out of the gum.
- You can see a break-line running up the tooth.
- There's a blog of flesh (dental pulp) sticking out.
- Your child is overly distraught.

Your dentist visit can wait until the next day when:

- The tooth has a crack.
- There's a chipped tooth.
- A tooth is pushed into the gum but nothing broke off and there's no bleeding.
- A tooth has shifted.

Gum, Lip, or Tongue Injuries

Sometimes, an accident can cause injury to the gums, lip, or tongue. When any of these bleed, it can look quite gruesome and the amount of blood may come as quite a shock to you and your baby.

Here's some things you can do to calm your little one down and ease their pain.

If there are cuts on the gums or lips, apply pressure with a small bag of ice or cover the abrasion with wet gauze until the bleeding stops. Comfort your baby with lots of hugs and try to distract them from the pain by playing a game of peek-a-boo or singing a song together. If the bleeding stops and there's no severe gum damage, you won't need to take your baby for a dental checkup. However, if your little one experiences continuous pain in that area, visit the dentist.

If your baby's tongue has been cut, don't panic—there will be a good amount of blood. The blood supply to the human tongue is pretty exceptional so it comes as no surprise that your baby will look like they belong in a horror movie. Even though your little one's tongue is causing a lot of drama, it will usually heal itself without any intervention. You only need to go to the doctor or the emergency room if the bleeding doesn't stop.

Baby Tooth Decay

It doesn't mean that because your little one's baby teeth will later be replaced by adult teeth that you don't have to worry about cavities. Tooth decay can be very uncomfortable for your little one and can result in pain and infection. Moreover, decayed baby teeth may impair the growth of your baby's adult teeth.

Don't take oral hygiene for granted and make an effort to prevent baby tooth decay.

- Avoid giving your little one beverages that are high in sugar, including juice and soda.
- Don't dip your baby's pacifier in sugar or syrup—it may lead to cavities in the top and bottom front teeth.
- Only place breast milk, formula, or cow's milk in your baby's bottle. Make sure they finish all the contents in the bottle before

bed or naptime to prevent baby bottle rot where natural sugars from the milk or formula cling to your baby's teeth for a long time. The bacteria in the mouth live on this sugar and will produce acids that attack your little one's teeth.

- Brush your child's teeth twice a day.

Luckily, it is never too late to start good dental hygiene habits. If you notice that a baby tooth is starting to rot, take your child to the dentist to get some personalized advice.

SEPARATION ANXIETY

Almost all children will go through a phase where they don't want to be separated from their mommy or daddy. It's a normal part of their emotional development and your little one will probably gain back their self-reliance when they're about two years old.

Separation anxiety usually kicks in around the eight-month mark but even babies as young as four months may experience it. When babies start to realize that objects and people still exist even though they can't see them (object permanence) there is a possibility that they may develop separation anxiety. For example, from four months, your baby will figure out that you don't disappear into thin air when you leave the room. This realization may lead to your little one becoming upset when they can't see you. Also, considering that your baby's concept of time only develops when they're older, they won't know when or if you'll return and this may cause a lot of waterworks.

During the separation anxiety phase, your baby will:

- Tense up around strangers and act shy around people they know and see often.
- Cry or put up a fuss whenever you leave the room or when you leave them with someone else.
- Cry when you leave them in the crib until you return.
- Wake up in the middle of the night and cry because you're not there.

How long will this continue for? As with everything else, each baby has their own timeline. That being said, it will be the worst between ten and 18 months. The length of time this phase continues will be affected by how you respond—if you run to your baby's rescue during each crying spell, you're teaching your little one that crying equals you coming back into the room. I know you want to comfort your baby when they're upset, but sometimes it's better to block out their crying to prevent future behavior that will do them more harm.

To take some of the stress off of you and your little one, here are some steps you can take to help you cope with this phase in your baby's life.

Plan when you leave. Go at a time when your baby is calm—after nap time or when they've been fed. Your little one is more prone to separation anxiety when they're hungry, tired, or feel ill. If they're sick, spend a lot of time with them to prevent unnecessary stress on your baby.

Don't make a fuss. If you give your baby to their caretaker or the babysitter, ask them to distract your little one with a toy while you slip away unnoticed.

Practice separation. There will be times when your baby will crawl into another room. When that happens, don't follow them right away, instead, give them some space. If you're worried about your child's safety in the other room, go check but leave the room after you've made sure it is safe for them to be there. Be sure to tell them you're going to the next room. If they cry after you leave, call to him as a form of comfort, but don't return right away. In time, your little one will learn that nothing bad will happen when you're not close.

Start an exit ritual. Don't just rush out the door when you drop your baby off at daycare or a sitter's. Take some time to play with them before you slip away. Before you go, tell them that you'll be back for them later in the day—giving them a specific time will be a bonus.

Keep your promise. If you told your baby you'll be back at lunchtime, make sure you return when you said you would. This will build your child's confidence that they'll survive the time apart since they can trust you to get them when you say you will.

Nighttime Separation Anxiety

Leaving your baby alone in their room while you know they're feeling anxious can be challenging. And hearing your baby cry in the middle of the night because you weren't next to them when they wake up can be soul destroying.

Separation anxiety is trying and exhausting even during the daytime, having to deal with it during the night adds another dimension to the situation. Thankfully, it won't take too long for your little one to realize that you'll still be there in the morning.

Until then, here are some tactics to help you lessen your baby's separation anxiety at night.

- Create a bedtime routine.
- Leave your baby's room door open.
- Give your baby an object they find comforting—their favorite blankie or stuffed animal will do.
- Don't reward their bad behavior by running to their rescue when they cry for you.

BOW LEGS

You're more worried about your child's legs than they are. If you see your little one's legs curve outward at the knees, while the feet and ankles touch, then your baby has bow legs. It's rarely serious —it's common under infants and toddlers, and will usually go away without treatment.

Bow legs don't bother children since it doesn't cause any discomfort or pain; it also doesn't affect your baby's ability to crawl, walk, or run. As a mom, you may worry about the appearance of your baby's legs, or about their awkward walking pattern, but these problems generally go away as your child grows.

Another common sign of bow legs is when your tiny tot walks with their toes pointed inward (intoeing) and may appear clumsy as they trip over seemingly anything. But again, this issue will resolve itself by age three or four.

But what exactly causes bow legs?

It happens because your baby had to fit into a tiny space while they were growing in your womb. This forced some of the bones to twist slightly and, consequently, your little one was born with what is called physiologic bow legs. But it's not as bad as it sounds (or looks), it's actually considered a normal part of a baby's growth and development.

When your baby starts walking, you may see an increase in the bowing, followed by it getting significantly better. Bow legs will also be more noticeable in those little one's who start walking at a young age. While most kids have an outward curve of the legs, some might have an inward curve (knock-knees).

Legs with an outward curve will correct on their own by age three or four, while knock-knees will straighten by age seven or eight.

It happens very rarely that bow legs are caused by underlying medical conditions, such as:

Rickets: A bone growth problem caused by a lack of vitamin D or calcium. It's more common in third-world countries where children do not get enough foods fortified with vitamin D. Rickets can also run in families thanks to a genetic problem that influences how the body uses vitamin D.

Blount disease: A growth disorder.

Injury, infection, or a tumor: Any condition that affects bone growth.

The most important thing you should know about bow legs is that your child doesn't need to limit their activities—they can run, walk, and play with their peers without any concern.

THINKING ABOUT ANOTHER BABY?

Pregnancy spacing is about more than choosing how far apart your children are in age. Family planning takes on a new meaning when you already have a child. Will you be able to take care of a newborn for the second time, how will the new baby affect your other child or children, are you financially secure enough to raise more than one kid? You have a lot of things to consider before deciding to get pregnant again.

The timing of your pregnancies also needs to be taken into account. Research shows that the length of the interval between giving birth and getting pregnant directly relates to the risk of infant, child, and maternal mortality (Starbird & Crawford, 2019).

Getting pregnant too early after giving birth increases your baby's risk of:

- Premature birth
- Placental abruption
- Congenital disorders
- Low birth weight
- Schizophrenia
- Autism

And the mother may experience maternal anemia.

If you think about it, your body needs more than six or even twelve months to recover from the previous pregnancy. Not only did growing a baby for nine months deplete all your body's stores of nutrients, but breastfeeding is also taking a good chunk of your reserves. If you become pregnant before you have time to build up nutrients in your body, it could negatively affect your health and your baby's health.

But what if you wait too long? There are some concerns when the period between pregnancies exceeds five years. For one, research shows that women have an increased risk of preeclampsia when there is a long interval between pregnancies—even with no history of the condition (Skjaerven, Wilcox & Lie, 2002). So, what's the best interval between pregnancies?

According to the Starbird & Crawford study cited earlier, waiting 18 to 24 months but less than five years after giving birth is the sweet spot. However, if a woman's biological clock is running out of time, she might consider waiting only 12 months before attempting her next pregnancy.

In the end, choosing when to have your next baby is you and your partner's personal decision. Together, you can weigh up the pros and cons and consider the various factors related to bringing another child into this world. But until you make your final decision, use a reliable form of birth control to prevent an 'oopsie.'

YOUR BABY'S FIRST BIRTHDAY!

*I*t's hard to believe but that tiny bundle of joy you brought home 12 months ago is turning one. Happy birthday, little one—you have now graduated from baby to toddler.

I can hear you sigh and ask, "Where did the time go?" I know, right? It seems like only yesterday that we started this journey.

Your baby's first birthday is a big milestone in their life; they're a toddler now and are approaching the terrible twos, threes, and, well, fours.

Here's what you can expect this month as your baby completes their first trip around the sun.

When it comes to communication, your soon-to-be one-year-old is a whiz at speaking without words. It's like you raised a resourceful little Neanderthal who grunts in response to your questions, stomps into the kitchen and points to a drink, or pushes your legs in the direction of the door when they want to go play outside.

Although your little one can speak only five or so recognizable words, you're more than able to understand exactly what they want. Relish your tot's attempt to communicate with you—before you know it, they'll be a teenager slamming the door in your face!

Even though your baby's skills have advanced speedily, the same can't be said about their attention span.

To stay sane, you have to recognize age-appropriate limitations—your little one isn't capable of sitting still for too long. Their focus is all over the place, so don't expect them to finish a puzzle in one sitting or listen to a story patiently. Whatever you do, don't force your baby to stay interested in something for longer periods; this will come with age. Instead, make play-time fun and interesting, while allowing your baby to develop vital skills.

Here are some things to keep in mind:

There's no need to buy your 12-month-old big-ticket items. In fact, your toddler will play with just about anything, even household items like kitchen utensils and bowls. If you do want to get them a new toy, grab some soft blocks or other stackable toys to keep them busy while also improving their coordination and motor skills.

Your baby is not too old for a game of peek-a-boo. It will still provide them with endless entertainment and will further develop their understanding of object permanence. It's a simple game but has a lot of benefits to your baby's development.

Restrict your little one's screen time. Turn off the television, put away any digital devices, and spend some quality one-on-one time with your baby.

I have some good news when it comes to your baby's diet: cow's milk is on the menu! Your baby is now old enough to enjoy this creamy drink without any negative consequences—assuming they don't turn out to be lactose intolerant, of course. So, replace their formula or add it to your baby's diet even while you're breastfeeding. Your growing tot can do with the extra vitamin D. When it comes to the type of milk, whole milk is the one you should go for. Your baby needs the extra fat for that fast-developing brain of theirs. Your baby needs to consume about 1,000 calories a day—half of these should come from breast milk, formula, or cow's milk. The only time I recommend you give your toddler reduced-fat milk is if obesity is a concern. Now, moo-ve it, go get your little one some cow's milk!

IT'S PARTY TIME

There are more than 31 million seconds in a year—doesn't feel like it if you look at how fast the year went by. Even though you're sticking to your story: your little one was only born yesterday, it is time for you to start planning their birthday party. There's no better way to celebrate all the developmental milestones they reached this year.

If this is your first child then planning a birthday party is going to leave you feeling excited and stressed at the same time. There's a lot to think about and even more things to juggle at once, and numerous things to tick off of your to-do list.

I don't want to brag, but with raising three kids, I consider myself somewhat of a pro birthday party planner. Let me share with you some helpful tips to make this event one to remember.

1. Keep the guest list small

Where older kids may want all of their twenty friends to attend the party, your baby doesn't really know what is going on. If you invite too many people, the hustle and bustle may startle them and spoil their special day. Keep your baby happy and smiling by making their first birthday party an intimate affair.

2. Don't disregard your baby's schedule

There are mealtimes and naps to consider when you plan your baby's party. It won't be a good idea to plan the party in the afternoon when you know this is the time your little one is extra fussy. Instead, plan the party in the morning when they're fresh out of bed, had breakfast, and are ready to entertain everyone with their bright personality. Furthermore, keep the party short. You know how your baby gets when they don't take their morning and afternoon naps, so limit the party to two hours. That's more than enough time to serve the cake, take photos, and enjoy some playtime before taking a nap.

3. Send out invitations

You want everyone to know your little one is the star of the event. The best way to do this is to include a photo of your baby on the invitation. You also want to include other important information like the date, time, place, and duration of the party.

4. Make sure the party area is baby-friendly

If your house is already baby proofed, then you don't have much to worry about. However, if you're having the party outdoors or at a new location, you'll have to get down on your hands and knees to look for any potential safety hazards. Even after you've scoured the place for possible dangers, always make sure there is someone to keep an eye on the young guests. You never know if you missed something that turns out to be a choking hazard.

Talking about safety, plastic or paper cups and tableware are better suited to kids' parties than glass.

5. Choose a theme

This is one of my favorite parts—it's fun and gives you a clear vision of what you plan to do. Keep in mind that the theme you choose will set the tone for the party. Also, dressing up your baby to fit the theme of the party is adorable and will make for great photos. What do you think about a tiny Cookie Monster digging into a birthday cake that is decorated like a big cookie? Sounds like a great idea to me!

6. Shop for fun and bright decorations

Remember, your baby and their guests love colorful, shiny, and moving objects. Use streamers, balloons, stuffed animals, and anything else you can think of that will turn their environment into a magical wonderland.

7. Don't forget about the adults

I know the party will only last a few hours but your adult guests will appreciate snacks and drinks while they are there. Of course you'll offer kid-friendly snacks—it's a birthday party after all, but a lot of parents forget about the adults. If you think smartly, you'll be able to conjure up finger foods that double as kid and adult snacks.

8. Get two birthday cakes

We've all seen the adorable photos of babies digging into a small birthday cake with their hands. It's messy and hilarious—you'll want to take a lot of photos and videos. If you only buy one cake and give it to your little one to destroy, your guests won't have any cake to eat. You can decorate your baby's smash cake to fit the party theme, but don't have to go all out for the cake the guests will be eating.

9. Get a professional photographer

This is your baby's first birthday and you want to capture every moment of it—or at least the cake smash part. Alternatively, arrange a professional photo shoot of your baby and their cake on a separate date. If you prefer to do it that way, you can use your phone to take photos and videos throughout the event. You'll definitely get a good mix of photos you can later use for scrapbooking projects, etc. You can also encourage your guests to take photos that they can later forward to you.

10. Hire a babysitter

I know you don't want to run around looking after your baby and the other children at the party. Get someone else to do it. If you have a babysitter you use regularly, consider paying her to come mind the children. Not only will she make extra money, she'll be able to enjoy the festivities and all the yummy food and drink that go with it. Having someone to help look after the kids will free up your time and you can socialize with the other parents.

Above all, remember to enjoy the party—it's just as much a celebration of you as it is of your baby. Your little one has been alive for a whole year and this is just the beginning. I realize you'll worry about being a good host, but don't forget the reason behind the party: your baby. Don't fret over the little things that may not turn out as planned. Instead, enjoy the day with your baby, family, and friends—it's all about making memories.

CREATING LASTING MEMORIES

I treasure the photos of my three children. If you were to ask me what three things I would grab in the event of a fire, the photo albums, scrapbooks and other keepsakes documenting my children's lives would make the cut.

I highly suggest you go through the mountains of photos you took (don't try to deny it) and turn them into a lasting memory you can later pass on to your child. You can even make one specifically of your baby's first birthday—those smash cake photos will look great in a scrapbook.

Some ideas include creating a:

- Scrapbook
- Photobook
- Memory box

You can use the various keepsakes you've gathered thus far and create a scrapbook or memory box of their first year. Put their hospital ID bracelet from when they were born, the lock of hair you kept when they went for their first haircut, and any other unique keepsakes in a box—don't forget to add some snapshots of your baby and the rest of your family members! This will make a special gift when your little one becomes an adult.

LEAVE A 1-CLICK REVIEW!

I would be incredibly thankful if you could take just 60 seconds to write a brief review on Amazon, even if it's just a couple sentences!

SCAN QR CODE ABOVE OR VISIT LINK BELOW:
https://www.amazon.com/review/create-review/?&
asin=B08ZSJW5KZ&ie=UTF8&

CONCLUSION

Mommies, that brings us to the end of *Baby Turns One*. You made it to the one-year mark and before you know it you'll be bragging about how you survived the terrible twos. Being a mother comes easier than most women initially think—we just have what it takes to care for a tiny human being. I hope you're proud of yourself. You and your baby experienced a lot of developmental milestones this year and where *Baby Turns One* focused on the first six months, this book guided you further, up until your baby's first birthday.

The biggest changes your little one went through the last six months are their transition to solid foods, weaning (if you chose to do so), teething, talking, sitting up alone, crawling, and walking. That's a lot of growth in a short time and you were there right beside them to cheer them on and catch them when they fall.

Of course, there are babies who are late bloomers, so I won't be surprised if some of you are still waiting for your baby to reach some of these milestones. And you know what, that's perfectly fine—as I said throughout this book, each baby has their own time-line. If you're truly worried that your baby is lagging too far behind, have a chat with their doctor and hear what they think.

So, what's next?

Well, your child's development is continuing at a steady pace. In their first year as a fully-fledged toddler, they can start to explore their creative side. If they don't already have some basic art supplies, consider getting them some. Your little one has the urge to doodle, so allow them to do so to their heart's content. This is a great way to develop their hand strength and learn how to control their fingers. However, you may want to keep a close eye on your budding Picasso, they may get so excited that they decide to draw you a mural on the wall!

Remember how your baby started to use non-verbal communication in month 12? This ability is going to go into overdrive from now on, especially when it comes to finger-pointing! Your tiny tot will enjoy getting your attention by pointing at random things. It's their way of saying, "Hey mom, I want you to look at what I'm looking at!" This is what experts call "shared attention" and it is a sign that your baby is developing as they should.

In general, pre-talkers are clever at inventing ways to communicate with you, and all forms of non-verbal communication are cause for celebration and require a response.

When it comes to your little one zooming around in the house, don't expect that to change anytime soon —it is actually going to get far worse. Your little one isn't so little anymore and is gaining confidence with every step they take. Walking will soon progress to running, and they'll throw jumping and climbing into the mix because they apparently want to give you an early heart attack!

Moving around like this takes a lot of practice—your tot needs to coordinate many movements to success-fully run, jump, or climb. It's your job as their mommy to encourage them, even when you're afraid they'll fall and break something. Keep telling yourself that these more daring moves build motor skills, but also teaches your little one coordination.

But here's when you can expect things to get a little wild:

Climbing: Although pulling themselves into a standing position can technically be considered 'climbing,' babies won't monkey around on the playground until they're at least one year old. Even then, some toddlers won't climb at playgrounds until around 24 months.

Running: Some toddlers pick up speed at around 13 months but, in general, you can expect your little one to start running at 17 months.

Kicking: Your little tot may love to kick toys around from time to time, but they don't have the gross motor coordination to kick a ball while standing. This is a skill they will only develop between 18 and 24 months.

Jumping: Not only will your little one need a lot of coordination and strength, they'll also have to be brave enough to take the leap. Before your baby attempts to jump, they will first take their itty-bitty body for a test drive to figure out what it can do. They'll start off with small, seemingly simple tasks like shifting their weight from one foot to another and then progress to jumping off of low structures until they have enough courage to jump on and off the bed! It's fascinating how they develop these skills!

It should be clear to you by now that there is a fun time ahead—and maybe a visit or two to the emergency room for some stitches. That's the reality of the matter: it doesn't matter how vigilant you are when it comes to your toddler's safety, they're very serious about exploring the world and this includes getting a few bumps and bruises along the way. Talking from personal experience, I spent a lot of time cleaning wounds and sticking on bandaids when my kiddies were still toddlers. And as expected, boys tend to be a little wilder than girls. I'm not trying to scare you—but prepare you. You have to let your kid be a kid for them to develop and reach the coming milestones. Believe me, they don't break easily, so you can make yourself a cup of tea and relax even when they're hanging upside down from the lowest branch of a tree in your backyard.

I hope the information in this book was of value to you. My aim with all the books I write is to educate mothers in such a way that they feel comfortable in their ability to raise happy and healthy children. If this book gave you the confidence to relax into your journey as a mother a little more, then I am beyond happy. Being a mother is such a great adventure and beyond that, a privilege—I don't want you to be held back by your fears.

MOMMY CHECKLIST

14 Baby Essentials Every Mom Must Have...

This checklist includes:

- 14 ESSENTIALS THAT YOU DIDN'T KNOW YOU NEEDED FOR YOUR LITTLE ONE AND YOURSELF
- ITEMS WHICH WILL MAKE BEING A MAMA BEAR EASIER
- WHERE YOU CAN PURCHASE THESE ITEMS AT THE LOWEST PRICE

The last thing you want to do is be unprepared and unequipped to give your little one an enjoyable and secure environment to grow up in. It is never too late to prepare for this!

To receive your free Mommy Checklist, visit the link or scan the QR code below:

https://purelypublishing.activehosted.com/f/1

ABOUT THE AUTHOR

Elizabeth Newbourne is an established nutritionist and loving mother of three. She has devoted her life to helping mothers understand how to take care of themselves and their little ones, both inside the womb during pregnancy and outside, as they guide their newborns through the developmental stages of life.

It is her passion to share with you everything she has learned from bringing into the world her two wonderful boys and her sweet little girl, as well as her two decades of knowledge in physical and psychological health and nutrition. She has coached and guided countless women through their pregnancies and helped mothers become the best version of themselves for their newborns and families, giving them access to the information she wishes she had when she was a new mother.

Her knowledge as a respected nutritionist, combined with her personal experience as a mother, makes her one of the leading experts on healthy and happy pregnancies and motherhood.

JOIN THE COMMUNITY:
www.facebook.com/groups/modernsupermom
www.instagram.com/elizabethnewbourne
elizabeth@newbornepublishing.com

REFERENCES

Badihian, S., Adihian, N., & Yaghini, O. (2017). The Effect of Baby Walker on Child Development: A Systematic Review. Iranian journal of child neurology, 11(4), 1–6

Beauchamp, G., Mennella, J. (2009). Early flavor learning and its impact on later feeding behavior. Journal of Pediatric Gastroenterology and Nutrition, 48(1). https://doi.org/10.1097/MPG.0b013e31819774a5

Beauregard, J.L., Bates, M., Cogswell, M.E., Nelson, J.M. & Hamner, H.C. (2019). Nutrient content of squeeze pouch foods for infants and toddlers sold in the United States in 2015. Nutrients, 11(7):1689. https://doi.org/10.3390/nu11071689

Bloomfield, S. F., Stanwell-Smith, R., Crevel, R. W., & Pickup, J. (2006). Too clean, or not too clean: the hygiene hypothesis and home hygiene. Clinical and experimental allergy : journal of the British Society for Allergy and Clinical Immunology, 36(4), 402–425. https://doi.org/10.1111/j.1365-2222.2006.02463.x

Carstairs, S.A., Craig, L., Marais, D., Ourania, E.B. & Kirsty, K. (2016). A comparison of preprepared commercial infant feeding meals with home-cooked recipes. Archives of Disease in Childhood, 101:1037-1042. https://adc.bmj.com/content/101/11/1037.info

Coulthard, H., Harris, G. & Emmett, P. (2009). Delayed introduction of lumpy foods to children during the complementary feeding period affects child's food acceptance and feeding at 7 years of age. Matern Child Nutr, 5(1):75-85. https://doi.org/10.1111/j.1740-8709.2008.00153.x

Coulthard, H., Williamson, I., Palfreyman, Z. & Lyttle, S. (2017). Evaluation of a pilot sensory play intervention to increase fruit acceptance in preschool children. Appetite, 1;120:609-615. https://doi.org/10.1016/j.appet.2017.10.011

Dahl, A., Campos, J. J., Anderson, D. I., Uchiyama, I., Witherington, D. C., Ueno, M., Poutrain-Lejeune, L., & Barbu-Roth, M. (2013). The epigenesis of wariness of heights. Psychological science, 24(7), 1361–1367. https://doi.org/10.1177/0956797613476047

Dazeley, P. & Houston-Price, C. (2014). Exposure to foods' non-taste sensory properties: A nursery intervention to increase children's willingness to try fruit and vegetables. Appetite, 84:1-6. https://doi.org/10.1016/j.appet.2014.08.040

Dettwyler, K. (2004). When to wean: Biological versus cultural perspectives. Clin Obstet Gyecol, 47(3), 712-723. https://doi.org/10.1097/01.grf.0000137217.97573.01

Dewar, G. (n.d.). Prenatal learning: Do "pregnancy foods" affect babies' eating habits? Parenting Science. https://www.parentingscience.com/prenatal-learning-about-food.html

Dietary Guidelines Advisory Committee. 2020. Scientific Report of the 2020 Dietary Guidelines Advisory

Committee: Advisory Report to the Secretary of Agriculture and the Secretary of Health and Human Services. U.S. Department of Agriculture, Agricultural Research Service. https://www.dietaryguidelines.gov/2020-advisory-committee-report

Figure 10: Menegay, M. (2017). Baby's feet [Photograph]. Unsplash. https://unsplash.com/photos/UojxG_BJxnI

Figure 11: McCucheaon, S. (2018). Baby beside green textile [Photograph]. Unsplash. https://unsplash.com/photos/5BRIjMTKFkU

Figure 12: Fore, P. (2017). Girl sitting on green grass field holding green fruit [Photograph]. Unsplash. https://unsplash.com/photos/miAcjhLaWPQ

Figure 13: Zhou, M. (2018). Baby sleeping on pillow [Photograph]. Unsplash. https://unsplash.com/photos/Tr7dT5m-SyI

Figure 14: Freestocks. (2017). Black cupcake [Photograph]. Unsplash. https://unsplash.com/photos/qlS6vMR2PpU

Figure 15: Fields, R. (2017). Boy playing cube on white wooden table [Photograph]. Unsplash. https://unsplash.com/photos/Xz7MMD5tZwA

Figure 16: Seaman, A. (2018). Toddler holding white camera toy [Photograph]. Unsplash. https://unsplash.com/photos/oDDsnKoYKVU

Figure 1: Encalada, J. (2019). Baby on bed [Photograph]. Unsplash. https://unsplash.com/photos/2BalskDOoLg/info

Figure 2: Hermann, C. (2019). Toddler boy in highchair [Photograph]. Unsplash. https://unsplash.com/photos/mpr5QrN9rjM/info

Figure 3: Yung, T. (2020). Person holding orange fruit with blackberries [Photograph]. Unsplash. https://unsplash.com/photos/h2dwDgbZM1Q

Figure 4: Braun, L. (2019). Woman carries baby [Photograph]. Unsplash. https://unsplash.com/photos/hdmGreHJPZ8

Figure 6: Dummer, A. (2017). Baby trying to get out of his crib [Photograph]. Unsplash. https://unsplash.com/photos/x4jRmkuDImo/info

Figure 7: Vanooteghem, J. (2017). Child playing on carpet [Photograph]. Unsplash. https://unsplash.com/photos/zpQpn5N1na8

Figure 8: Ridao, R. (2018). Person feeding baby from feeding bottle [Photograph]. Unsplash. https://unsplash.com/photos/TCYj_UxoIUY

Figure 9: Bertrand, M. (2016). Toddler girl wearing teal and white polka dot long sleeve shirt and white tutu skirt outfit walking on green sod at daytime [Photograph]. Unsplash. https://unsplash.com/photos/eyzzqAQhcjI

Figure5: Spanic, L. (2020). White and black short coated dog lying on brown wooden floor [Photograph]. Unsplash. https://unsplash.com/photos/uCT59SrYwbY

Forestell, C. A., & Mennella, J. A. (2017). The Relationship between Infant Facial Expressions and Food Acceptance. Current nutrition reports, 6(2), 141–147. https://doi.org/10.1007/s13668-017-0205-y

Gottlieb, S. (2000). Early exposure to cows' milk raises risk of diabetes in high risk children. BMJ : British Medical Journal, 321(7268), 1040. https://

www.ncbi.nlm.nih.gov/pmc/
articles/PMC1173447/

Gross, B.A. (1991). Is the lactational amenorrhea method a part of natural family planning? Biology and policy. Am J Obstet Gynecol, 165(6 Pt 2), 2014-9. https://doi.org/10.1016/s0002-9378(11)90571-7

Gupta, R.S., Warren, C.M., Smith, B.M., Blumenstock, J.A., Jiang, J., Davis, M.M & Nadeau, K.C. (2018). The Public Health Impact of Parent-Reported Childhood Food Allergies in the United States. Pediatrics, 142 (6).https://doi.org/10.1542/peds.2018-1235

Healthline. (n.d.). What is extrusion reflex? https://www.healthline.com/health/parenting/extrusion-reflex

Hepper, P.G., Wells, D.L. & Lynch C. (2005). Prenatal thumb sucking is related to postnatal handedness. Neuropsychologia, 43(3), 313-5. https://doi.Org/10.1016/j.neuropsychologia.2004.08.009

Leung, A. K., & Sauve, R. S. (2003). Whole cow's milk in infancy. Paediatrics & child health, 8(7), 419–421. https://doi.org/10.1093/pch/8.7.419

Medela. (n.d.). Breastfeeding beyond six months: What are the benefits? https://www.medela.com/breastfeeding/mums-journey/breastfeeding-beyond-6-months#reference

Moding, K.J., Feraante, M.J., Bellows, L.L., Bakke, A.J., Hayes, J.H. & Johnson, S.L. (2018). Variety and content of commercial infant and toddler vegetable products manufactured and sold in the United States. The American Journal of Clinical Nutrition, 107(4), 576–583. https://doi.org/10.1093/ajcn/nqx079

Nielsen's Total Food View. (2018). Total Consumer Report 2018. https://www.nielsen.com/wp-content/uploads/sites/3/2019/04/total-consumer-report-june-2018.pdf

Ocklenburg, S., Schmitz, J., Moinfar, Z., Moser, D., Klose, R., Lor, S., Kunz, G., Tegenthoff, M., Faustmann, P., Franks, C., Epplen J.T., Kumsta, R. & Gunturkun, O. (2017). Epigenetic regulation of lateralized fetal spinal gene expression underlies hemispheric asymmetries.eLife,6:e22784. https:// doi.org/10.7554/eLife.22784

Oddy, W.H., Kendall, G.E., Li, J., Jacoby, P., Robinson, M., de Klerk, N.H., Silburn, S.R., Zubrick, S.R., Landau, L.I. & Stanley, F.J. The long-term effects of breastfeeding on child and adolescent mental health: A pregnancy cohort study followed for 14 years. J Pediatr, 156(4):568-74. https://doi.org/10.1016/j. jpeds.2009.10.020

Pfeiffer, M., Kotz, R., Ledl, T., Hauser, G. & Sluga, M. Prevalence of flat foot in preschool-aged children. Pediatrics, 118(2):634-9. https:/doi.org/10.1542/peds.2005-2126

Skjaerven, R., Wilcox, A.J. & Lie, R.T. (2002). The interval between pregnancies and the risk of preeclampsia. N Engl J Med, 346:33-38. https://doi. org/10.1056/NEJMoa011379

Starbird, E., & Crawford, K. (2019). Healthy Timing and Spacing of Pregnancy: Reducing Mortality Among Women and Their Children. Global health, science and practice, 7(Suppl 2), S211–S214. https://doi.org/10.9745/GHSP-D-19-00262

The American Academy of Pediatrics. (n.d.). Infant food and feeding. https://www.aap.org/en-us/advocacy-and-policy/aap-health-initiatives/HALF-Implementation-Guide/Age-Specific-Content/Pages/Infant-Food-and-Feeding.aspx

Wolf, S., Simon, J., Patikas, D., Schuster, W., Armbrust, P. & Döderlein, L (2008). Foot motion in children shoes: A comparison of barefoot walking with shod walking in conventional and flexible shoes. Gait & Posture, 27(1), 51-9. https://doi.org/10.1016/j.gaitpost.2007.01.005

World Health Organisation. (2020). Infant and young child feeding. https://www.who.int/news-room/fact-sheets/detail/infant-and-young-child-feeding#:~:text=WHO%20and%20UNICEF%20recommend%3A,years%20of%20age%20or%20beyond

Yu, C., Binns, C. W., & Lee, A. H. (2019). The Early Introduction of Complementary (Solid) Foods: A Prospective Cohort Study of Infants in Chengdu, China. Nutrients, 11(4), 760. https://doi.org/10.3390/nu11040760

Printed in Great Britain
by Amazon

44773741R00118